The Nanny State

First published in Great Britain in 2004
by Artnik
341b Queenstown Road
London SW8 4LH
UK

ISBN 1 903906 50 4

Illustrator: Adam Berry
Design: Mark Lloyd

Printed and bound in Spain by Zubi

The Nanny State

Robert Huntington

ARTNIK

With special thanks to Henry Morton Jack, Harry Acton, Valentina and Artnik's Golden Retriever, Lucky, who would always take me for a walk when Nanny became too strict.

Robert Huntington

CONTENTS

Nanny knows best

'Englishmen never will be slaves: they are free to do whatever the Government and public opinion allow them to do.'

George Bernard Shaw

The first week of August 2003 saw temperatures in Britain soaring to record-breaking levels, at one point, on the sixth, reaching 39.5C at Gravesend in Kent, the highest recorded temperature for nearly fifteen years.

The schools were on vacation, there was a bank holiday weekend, there wasn't a cloud in the sky, the flowers were in bloom, and the English countryside shimmered at its most spectacular. Barbecues sizzled in gardens, the shrieks of children playing echoed through parks, toasts were proposed over glasses of Pimm's, ice creams melted onto beach towels, and lovers strolled together, aimlessly celebrating life. Everybody was happy and all was well with the world.

Or so it seemed.

In a gloomy, air-conditioned office in Whitehall, an urgent meeting was called. Around a large table were gathered some of the leading experts of the 'caring' services. At one point, a woman, overcome by the enormity of what was under discussion, burst into tears and hurried from the room. At intervals various doom-laden predications were made. 'Thousands will die.' 'The hospitals will not be able to cope.' 'Children!' 'The Disabled!' 'THE ELDERLY!'

The chairperson of the meeting eventually calmed the assembled company down. They were here to save the nation, she reminded them, and must not set a bad example by panicking. The group gradually regained its composure, and got to work. Saving the world was a tough, sometimes thankless task, but somebody had to do it. At the end of the meeting, the Department of Health issued the following grave instructions to the nation:

STAY INDOORS

If you CANNOT AVOID being out in the sun
apply sunscreen (factor 15+) and wear a shirt, hat and sunglasses.

VENTILATE YOUR HOME
Keep some windows open all day and all night. However, **BE CAREFUL**, because burglars will use open windows to get in.

LOOK AFTER THE ELDERLY

Older people are more prone to the effects of heat. Help them to keep as cool as possible, using a fan if necessary.

PROTECT CHILDREN
A good way to check if they are drinking enough is that they are passing urine regularly and that it is not too dark. You should check nappies regularly. Babies and the very young **MUST** be kept out of the sun.

AVOID PHYSICAL EXERTION

AVOID THE PERILS OF OUTDOOR EATING
Warm summer weather is a breeding ground for bacteria so it is especially important to keep hot foods hot and cold foods cold until you are ready to eat them. If you must barbecue, make sure you cook meat until it is piping hot, none of it is pink and all juices run clear.

Away from Whitehall, however, the barbecues continued to sizzle, the children continued to play, the lovers continued to stroll and the ice creams continued to melt. A few chuckles, perhaps, could be heard at the Department of Health's expense; there may even, for those few who bothered to think further about this patronsing nonsense, have been the occasional musing about the amount wasted on funding such pointless exercises. Otherwise, however, life continued as it should under the blazing summer sun.

The term 'Nanny State' was coined in 1979 by Margaret Thatcher who warned:

> We should not expect the state to appear in the guise of an extravagant good fairy at every christening, a loquacious companion at every stage of life's journey, and the unknown mourner at every funeral.

She declared her intention to rid Britain of the burgeoning Nanny State that she saw as the inevitable consequence of socialism and, instead, to replace it with an 'Enterprise Culture'. She succeeded in doing this but it also brought with it the capitalist excess of the eighties, with city wide boys in pinstriped suits and jaunty red braces popping their champagne corks and driving around in brightly coloured Lamborghinis. To her detractors, of course, such vulgar displays of material success highlighted a society where those who could not exploit the market found themselves saddled with the Poll Tax and lengthening queues for the dole.

The fresh breed of idealists responsible for the current mutation of the Nanny State, however, have accepted the idea that the economy can only effectively be run on capitalist lines, rather than attempting to develop a means by which all sectors of society could equally share the fruits of production. They have merely dreamed of ways that its excesses can supposedly be checked. It is here that the analogy between the state and a Nanny is most appropriate, as the state tells its children how to behave when faced with the terrors posed by the multinationals, punishes them if they eat too much or puff on a cigarette, stops them from calling each other nasty names, and, where anybody gets hurt, offers 'counselling' to soothe away the pain.

The idealists who were itching to establish a Nanny State had been forced to wait in the wings since 1979, only occasionally raising their collective voice to criticise Thatcherism before retreating again to bicker self-righteously with each other over who was the more 'radical'. Tony Blair's electoral victory in 1997 heralded a new era, an era in which the evils of 'Thatcherism' were to be cast aside, and a more 'caring' society was to be established. This fond hope was entertained by a variety of factions within the Labour Party, many of whose beliefs were diametrically opposed, but all of whom were united in a hatred of the 'establishment' that had run the country before them. They were also united in a desire to take far more direct control over the lives of the citizens they now governed.

The various factions were reconciled to each other under the mystical 'Third Way' – a political ideal that claimed to have resolved the differences between free-market capitalism and authoritarian collectivism. The magical formula was to allow a competition-driven economy, but with a social conscience. It would be achieved by checking big-business excesses with new legislation in the social sphere. The aim was to ban practices of which the social idealists disapproved. In 1999 two of the chief proponents of the 'Third Way', Tony Blair and Gerhard Schröder, issued a joint 'declaration' in which they announced, 'We support a market economy, not a market society.'

Suddenly, all those with a particular agenda to push – the politically-correct lobby, the 'rights' fanatics, the multiculturalists, the health and safety fascists, the child-care groups and other self-appointed guardians of public morality – were given free rein to lobby for their particular cause, and to start pressing for legislation to force the population to behave according to their various whims. The old assumption that people were generally best left to decide their own fate was swept away, and people were instead viewed as pathetic and rather needy. No longer were they the architects of their own lives, they were helpless pawns in a game over which they had no hope of gaining control. From now on, only Nanny could protect them from the marauding fat cats.

Thus, a quarter-century after Thatcher made her speech condemning the Nanny State, there is barely an aspect of life into which some civil servant or another has not poked his nose, found a problem, formed a committee, appointed a 'czar', organised a 'think tank', and announced an 'initiative' in order to solve it.

From the food that we eat, the drugs that we take, the sex that we have, through to the culture we consume and, therefore, to the very thoughts that we think, there is a governmental body which has declared an interest, procured funding for 'research', and issued instructions on how things should be done. As a result, those aspects of daily life that used to be considered private have been thrown open to the government's unwarranted intrusion, and a tangled mess of legislation has been introduced to keep bureaucrats in business and the public in line.

The ordinary citizen has responded to the government's unwarranted intrusions with bemusement. For example, most people were baffled rather than relieved to learn that the description

'English' has been deemed racist and that the flag of St. George is now considered so offensive that London taxi drivers are banned from displaying it. The continued attempt to sideline British tradition in order not to offend minorities is itself racist, and actually prevents those from immigrant traditions being embraced by their adopted country. Often, a dogmatic approach to multiculturalism leads to appalling displays of neglect and often aggravates the very problems that it seeks to solve. Frequently, too, the zealous pursuit of the ideal is simply ridiculous. There can hardly have been a pub in Birmingham, for example, which did not resound to the sound of drinkers, of all colours and creeds, laughing heartily at the pointless inanity of their City Council's decision to rename Christmas 'Winterval', in a bid to make the 'holiday period' more 'inclusive'.

Similarly, the relentless demands of political correctness, idealistically conceived to promote equality, have out-parodied Orwell's doublethink. The mistake of assuming that changing the way people are forced to speak in public affects the way they think in private becomes increasingly obvious the more the movement is lampooned. Replacing established, descriptive words such as 'blind', 'black' or 'old' with unnecessary and longwinded euphemisms is absurdly patronising, not least to the minority groups supposedly being protected. The constant tip-toeing around potentially offensive language could go on forever, and is now beyond the realms of parody. There can't have been a luvvie in the land, for example, who did not shrug his shoulders in bemused indifference at the news that the English National Opera, due to new government guidelines on sexual harassment, have had to ban their fawning divas from addressing each other as 'Darling' because the 'use of the word constitutes sexual harassment'.

Alongside this has come the almost religious zeal of the health and safety fanatics, whose influence over every sphere of public life has long since ceased to have any positive effect and has become a menace itself. They are constantly chivvying away at people's freedoms, increasing the extent to which the government or local councils can intrude into their lives. From the furious residents of the London borough of Kensington and Chelsea, where pubs and restaurants have been ordered to remove seating from the sides of pavements so that overexcited drinkers cannot fall into the path of oncoming traffic, through the schoolchildren of Derby who, having had suncream banned from the playground because of potential allergic reactions, have subsequently had school trips in the summer banned because of the threat of skin cancer to their unprotected bodies, to the managers of restaurants up and down the country who have had the quality of their creations compromised by idiotic requirements such as the one that cheese – whose taste develops as it matures – must be kept refrigerated, or that good beef – which is ruined by being over-cooked – must be cooked until no blood remains, there can barely be a group left in the country who have not had some previously essential liberty removed under the continued barrage of preposterous restrictions.

Meanwhile, the clamour of life in the Nanny State continues unabated with the incessant bleating of the anti-smoking, anti-hunting, anti-drinking, anti-drugs, anti-driving, and countless other lobbies softening us up to conform to what they believe is best for us.

The extent to which we are being bossed around by these meddling and almost entirely unelected busybodies has become so entrenched that most of us are resigned to it. We have begun to regard the avalanche of stories in the press detailing the Nanny State's latest wheeze with an amusement that borders on affection. The *Guardian*-reading army of 'Five-a-Day-Coordinators', 'Smoking Cessation Officers', 'Health and Safety Inspectors', as well as the little men proudly erecting 'Warning' signs everywhere or painting unnecessary brightly coloured lines all over the roads and pavements have taken on the status of loveable English eccentrics, in the tradition of such deluded anti-heroes as Basil Fawlty or David Brent.

Such amused toleration of the Nanny State, though, fails to recognise the fact that, sanctioned by this government and its almost totalitarian approach to the life of the citizen, it has far-reaching and potentially disastrous consequences.

The first, and most obvious effect, is the gradual restriction of personal freedom. A government this certain of how we should behave, naturally uses its legislative power to force us to conform. Through a manipulation of the judicial system, and a campaign of attrition, the population is being tricked into surrendering its liberty. It is being subjected to a relentless propaganda campaign and a systematic assault on truth and rational thought. Individuals cannot be trusted to decide for themselves how they should behave, so legislation is required to take responsibility away from them.

Not only is this form of thinking an affront to democracy and liberty, it is also manipulated to fit the agenda of those in power. They believe that as they have seen the light they are right to use their legislative authority to impose their vision upon us. With extraordinary frequency, however, the presumptions and figures on which much of this legislation is based are wrong, miscalculated, or simply lied about. You need look no further than the presentation of the case for war in Iraq to see how prepared ministers are to mislead us. Despite Blair's beloved weapons of mass destruction never being found, the war was still justified because Saddam was a bad man who would have used them if he'd had them. Similarly, when the Nanny State is shown up for exaggerating various threats to our health, the excuse is trotted out that lies and misrepresentation are used as part of a 'noble cause'. The government and its various quangos have a particular ideal of the environment in which they would have us live, and, therefore, are all too happy to disregard the truth in order to impose it upon us.

The second effect, the consequences of which will be felt for decades to come, is the toll that the expansion of the state will inevitably take on the economy. The present government delights in boasting of the rapid increase in employment, but it is worth considering how this miracle has been achieved. Over the last five years, 750,000 jobs have been created in public administration, health and education. We do not, however, have significantly greater numbers of policemen, doctors, teachers, or nurses – such jobs require training, expertise and commitment. The vast majority of the jobs created are those of managers, form-fillers, do-gooders and target-fiddlers – pointless bureaucratic posts that further burden the taxpayer and continue to strangle the public services.

The third effect is that the population is being, in Thatcher's word, 'coddled' into state dependence. Armies of extra social workers are constantly recruited to attend to the helpless masses, and the counselling industry has escalated beyond all decency as more and more of us are fooled into thinking that our problems are not our own and that only a 'professional' can help.

The Welfare State, instituted as a safety net for those who were in genuine need of the state's assistance, has been massively expanded by the Nanny State to further entrench people's reliance on her, and we are now in a preposterous position, with more than half of the population entitled to some form of handout. At first the idea of taking money from people in taxes and then returning a portion of it to them in welfare – losing a significant proportion of it to the bureaucrats employed to engineer such unnecessary reimbursement – might seem absurd, but it makes good political sense. It massively expands the class of people dependent on the government for a portion of their income, and it also mobilises an enormous army of semi-educated bureaucrats, who depend on the government for the whole of their income. When four out of ten voters are directly employed by the governing party, there is increasingly little danger of that party being voted out of office. Another party could only present a viable alternative by proposing to make a large percentage of the electorate redundant. Faced with the prospect of finding worthwhile means to earn a living, today's legion of time-wasting civil servants would inevitably stay loyal to Nanny.

We are rapidly becoming a nation infantilised, increasingly incapable of making informed choices for ourselves, no longer able to enjoy what life has to offer responsibly, and convinced that the smallest personal failing is the fault of vast external powers. Market forces dictate that as those who sign up to help the 'weak' and the oppressed increase, so the number of those requiring such help must expand. Thus, the ever growing catchment area for those who are labelled 'vulnerable', and the invention of ludicrous 'conditions' that require treatment. Taken to its logical conclusion, those that are fit to be considered medically sane will eventually constitute a minority.

The purpose of this book is to look at how the Nanny State has become such a parasitic, tax-sucking leech on our society, then to show that it is far more pervasive, embedded and pernicious than most of us realise, before finally examining its likely implications for our future.

As is argued above, many of the symptoms of the Nanny State seem harmless, and in many cases are actually very funny. It could be argued that the Nanny State is merely an inevitable over-reaction to the more destructive effects of Thatcher's 'detached' form of government. The alienating effects New Labour's adoption of Thatcher's economic policies are merely being counterbalanced by their zeal for interventionism. Perhaps the Nanny State and its philosophies represent nothing more than a political 'fad' which will soon be forgotten.

Sadly, this is unlikely. The most pernicious effects of the Nanny State will not be felt by the electorate, who have their own apathy and indifference to blame for its existence in the first place; the Nanny State's gravest legacy will felt by the electorate's children. They are growing up in such a sanitised and regulated environment that the world around them no longer seems to be a place of freedom and discovery. Their schoolrooms have become nothing more than battlegrounds for rival social doctrines, rather than places of education. The extent to which the Nanny State plans to take over the indoctrination of children is staggering. It is personified in the absurd but faintly sinister 'Minister for Children', Margaret Hodge, who quite seriously announced in 2003 that the upbringing of children 'cannot be abandoned to the vagaries of the individual'. Instead, the state must take direct control.

This grotesque prospect elevates the danger of the Nanny State well above that of a mere expensive irritant and, in an ironic twist that even Thatcher could never have predicted, makes the state a direct rival to parents for the upbringing of their own children.

In 2004, the 'Nanny State' has ceased to be a metaphor.

THE NANNY STATE

1 **Nanny's family tree**

This royal throne of kings, this sceptered isle,
Whose rocky shore beats back the envious siege
Of wat'ry Neptune, is now bound with shame,
With inky blots, and rotten parchment bonds.
That England that was wont to conquer others
Hath made a shameful conquest of itself.

William Shakespeare, *Richard II*, Act 2, Scene 1

Historically, the church provided the means for the governing classes to pass judgement on the private behaviour of the citizen. Whereas nowadays the population is deterred from the vices of sexual promiscuity and excessive alcohol consumption with warnings of 'Health-Risks' and 'Safety Hazards' in leaflets distributed by the HSE, it was once frightened into behaving itself with the threat of an eternity scorched by 'Hellfire and Brimstone' issued in solemn sermons on Sunday mornings.

The threat of such an uncomfortable-sounding eternity was almost as effective at keeping the peasants in line and away from the vices of sexual immorality and binge drinking, as it's now called, and for centuries the Church, under the auspices of the monarchy, maintained a reasonable discipline over the country. However, there was never, other than under the vague umbrella of religion, a coherent strategy behind the Church's disciplining of the congregation. Its authority was mainly wielded to keep the peasants from misbehaving and turning up drunk to Mass. In return for being offered spiritual guidance, the serfs were expected to make yearly payments to the church in the form of tithes, which generally comprised a tenth of their annual crop or animal production. That way the peasants were spared the terrors of certain damnation and the clergy were well fed and clothed in return for their piety. Such cynical self-interest was easily disguised from a population which couldn't read and still believed in goblins. But gradually Britain began educating itself.

By the Seventeenth century, the idea that a government should represent the interests of the people rather than the interests the monarch had taken hold sufficiently for a civil war to be fought over the matter. On one side, there was Parliament, representing 'the people' and their right to be treated fairly and, on the other, was King Charles I, representing himself and an expenses' budget fit for a king.

Unfortunately, the Parliamentary side was gradually brought under the control of Oliver Cromwell, a man who shared that most dangerous of Tony Blair's vices, idealism. The establishment of the Protectorate did, of course, set Britain on the road to democracy, in that Cromwell had demonstrated that the monarch was not the invincible and divinely-appointed ruler that the country had been led to believe. However, Cromwell, with his barely-repressed dictatorial tendencies, also shared Blair's understanding of 'representation', in that he believed he could govern on the people's behalf without caring what they wanted.

On 6 November, 1648, Cromwell declared his intention to implement an early form of enforced multiculturalism:

> ...I desire from my heart – I have prayed for – I have waited for this day to see – union and understanding between the godly people – Scots, English, Jews, Gentiles, Presbyterians, Anabaptists and all... Is it not fit to be civil, to profess love, to deal with clearness with the people for the removal of prejudices?

Precisely what 'prejudices' Cromwell felt authorised to 'remove' from the people have been debated by historians ever since, but it seems clear that some contemporaries were suspicious of his Utopian ambitions. A certain Scottish politician blessed with one of the great surnames in British politics, Robert Blair, stated on the same day that he found Cromwell to be '...an egregious dissembler, a great liar..and a greeting deevil'. Interestingly, the shortcomings he objected to in Cromwell's personality appear to be alive and well in his own family's descendants. This particular political Blair, however, had less effect on the country than our current Prime Minister because, despite his avowal that he would be prepared to go to the scaffold himself to stop Cromwell taking power, the Parliamentarians won, heralding in England's brief period as a republic. Robert Blair escaped execution, demonstrating a survival instinct that has, perhaps, remained in the gene pool

The execution of the reigning monarch in 1649 made for an especially dramatic start to Cromwell's Protectorate, and of ironic relevance to our current government's conviction that it is operating on our behalf, because a mass of contemporary evidence indicates that the British public did not support their King's state-endorsed death. Perhaps they were perceptive enough to appreciate even then that the one thing worse than an out-of-touch aristocracy lording it over a massively deprived nation would be a supposedly democratic government interfering with every aspect of their private lives in the name of progress.

Charles I, even by the standards of the Seventeenth century, had certainly been a selfish head of state with little concern for his subjects, but that very indifference guaranteed that he would never dream of banning dancing, theatre going and even Christmas celebrations in the name of a better future, as his successors did. The Protectorate, with the conviction of its architects' Puritanism, set about legislating immediately with a zeal that the present Nanny State can only envy. Pointless enjoyment was frowned upon. Cromwell's Parliament shut many inns, all the theatres, and most sports were banned. Boys caught playing football on a Sunday were whipped as a punishment. Swearing was punishable by a fine, and those that kept swearing after being fined were sent to prison.

Despite its obvious dissatisfaction with such a regime, the public were told they were getting what they needed, rather than what they wanted and, as such, the new republic could only live by rejecting every principle on which it had been professedly founded. Bradshawe, the sentencing judge at the King's trial, grandly declared that '...there is something superior to law, the parent or author of the law, and that is the people of England'. Worryingly, however, the people of England had no say in their government, which proceeded to 'represent' their interests in a way the current cabinet would no doubt find inspirational.

In February 1649 it abolished the House of Lords as '...unnecessary, burdensome and dangerous to the liberty, safety and public interests of the people of this nation'. The proposed constitutional upheavals of 2003 were couched by the government in similarly disingenuous terms, which also ignored the fact that the 'undemocratic' and 'unnecessary' House of Lords was often the only bastion of reason in an otherwise representative but utterly undemocratic Parliament.

Our present government is perpetually obsessed by the injustice of hereditary or unelected individuals possessing constitutional authority, yet almost every ministerial and constitutional position that is appointed by the Prime Minister rather than by the electorate or the party seems to be occupied by childhood friends, university flat-mates, former legal tutors, or current squash partners of Mr. Blair. An example of how appointments of Tony's cronies engender dangerous political arrogance is adequately supplied by Alastair Campbell, who behaved in the aftermath of the Hutton Report into the death of whisteleblower David Kelly as if it had been commissioned purely for his personal exoneration.

One of the deepest flaws in the concept of a Nanny State is that while it arises out of a professed desire to care responsibly for its citizens, it cannot help holding their opinions in a shocking degree of contempt. One of Cromwell's MPs, Henry Marten, was speaking exactly the same language as David Blunkett when he defended his government's policies in 1650 as '...a new experiment which must be nursed by the mother who brought it forth and can not yet be submitted to the rude winds of popular judgment'.

By the following year, Cromwell saw the people's rage at his government's experiment and accurately identified the cause:

> ...meddling in their private affairs, giving much ground for people to open their mouths against them and dislike them. Nor can they be brought within the bounds of justice and law or reason, they themselves being the supreme power of the nation, liable on no account to any, nor to be controlled or regulated by any other power.

Parliament certainly had the power to control and regulate others, however, not least in the form of one of its biggest money-spinners, on-the-spot fines for 'delinquents and ne'er-do-wells'. Nonetheless, even in the 1650s there were legal problems with the implementation of such policies, which the government overcame by setting up an unelected seventeenth-century version of a 'think tank' whose mission statement was '...to consider the inconveniences of the law, and the speediest way to remedy the same'. Cromwell took a mere four years to reach the same dangerous conclusion as Charles I, who had said on the scaffold that '...what the country longs for is good government, not self-government'.

The notion that a government should decide what is 'good' for us has such far-reaching implications because it implies that it knows better than we do. Even if it does, the main benefit of a liberated existence is the freedom to make mistakes and learn from them. If that essential quality of existence is removed, and the 'good' life is prescribed by government, it doesn't matter whether the arbiter of 'good' is a seventeenth-century Puritan or a twenty-first-century Christian ex-barrister – the result is the same for the people. Unelected individuals, hiding behind uncontrollable institutions, decide what is 'good' for us without caring whether we agree.

Cromwell's death in 1658 and the failure of his son to carry on where he left off led to the country asking Charles II to return to the throne on May 29, 1660. The country was overjoyed to have a monarch again after the Eleven Years Tyranny, although the lessons learned from the days of Charles I ensured that his royal powers and privileges were severely limited, and he was forced to fund his administration from customs duties and the allowance given to him by Louis XIV. In return, however, and mindful of his father's fate, Charles II was an extremely tolerant king and the country got back to normal, with theatres reopening and sports happily played again.

Despite the appearance of the country having come full circle, and the description of the events of 1660 as a 'Restoration', a profound and defining moment in English political history had actually taken place. Gone was the idea, central to the world view of the Tudor monarchs, of Royal prerogative, and for the first time Parliament had established itself as superior to the monarch. The modern concept of political parties was formed from the ashes of the Cavaliers and the Roundheads. As such, the Restoration can be seen as the first significant step in the forging of the modern state.

The temper of England has always been laissez-faire when it comes to government, and in the words of the great historian Macaulay, we look for success not to '...the intermeddling of an omniscient and omnipotent state, but to the prudence and energy of the people'. So long as in the last resort we have the right of interference we will be contentedly indifferent about most of the business of government. After the Restoration the merit of successive administrations was that they left the people alone, or at the most removed obstacles to their activity. In doing so, the growth of the state was largely a positive thing, as its development was now chained to improving the lives of the people, while not infringing on their liberty.

The first time that the state began to ask directly for contributions from the citizen was in 1799, when the Prime minister, William Pitt the Younger, announced the introduction of income tax to fund the Napoleonic wars. Once the idea of direct taxation was instituted, it was inevitably going to take hold permanently, although it was repealed on and off until 1842, when Sir Robert Peel reluctantly re-introduced as the only means of tackling a growing deficit. However, he only proposed to tax those whose incomes exceeded £150, which meant that the poor benefited from the system.

The introduction of a system of taxation was something that was essential to the development of the modern state, and had a practical benefit to the peasant class, unlike the tithe system operated by the Church. It also meant, though, that there was a reserve of money guarded by the state, whose duty it was, on the behalf of those who had contributed it, to ensure that it was used effectively.

Alongside the development of taxation had developed the idea that the state had to take some responsibility for combating the social ills that were the result of a successful economy. Contemptuously dismissed by Napoleon as a 'nation of shopkeepers', as a truly industrialised power Britain had developed into the 'workshop of the world'. One of the main economic factors that allowed for this was the adoption of laissez-faire policies with regard to the regulation of markets. The developing understanding of unregulated capitalism as a means to generate economic growth, increase employment and encourage competitiveness on an international stage was one that was gaining ground in social policy, and led to the development of the 'self-help' ideal, best articulated by its greatest contemporary advocate, Samuel Smiles, in 1859:

> Whatever is done for men or classes, to a certain extent takes away the stimulus and necessity of doing for themselves; and where men are subjected to over-guidance and over-government, the inevitable tendency is to render them comparatively helpless.

The fact that Smiles was actually a rather smug moralist, prone to fatuous platitudes such as 'Heaven helps those who help themselves' did not detract from the influence of his doctrine.

It was these same ideals of the self-help society that informed the politics of Margaret Thatcher, who called for a return to 'Victorian Values' as a way of turning around the country's ailing economy when she took power in 1979. By this she meant limiting the role of the state to prevent people from assuming that they could lie back and let it look after them while allowing businesses to operate unhampered by unnecessary bureaucracy.

Her aim to make Britain a more competitive trading nation was influenced heavily by the work of the political economist Adam Smith. In *The Wealth of Nations* (1776), he argued that by removing the traditional restrictions on trade imposed by nations in order to protect their own goods, nations would actually encourage their own producers and traders to operate more effectively by stimulating competition and innovation.

Smith's ideas influenced many Victorian Prime Ministers including Robert Peel, Benjamin Disraeli, and William Gladstone. Gladstone in particular was so opposed to the principle of direct taxation that he promised to abolish it if he won the 1874 election. He lost. Even so, the state remained very small, with only two per cent of all state expenditure going on the running of government departments. The Marxist historian Eric Hobsbawm wrote: 'By the middle of the nineteenth century government policy in Britain came as near laissez-faire as has ever been practicable in a modern state.' Contemporary opposition to the idea of a centralising state is succinctly summed up by Charles Dicken's character of Mr. Podsnap in *Our Mutual Friend*: 'Centralisation? No. Never with my consent. Not English.'

Despite such objection, there was a developing trend in political thought toward more state intervention in social matters, as the problems of the increased wealth of an industrialised society became evident. Between 1700 and 1900 the population increased fivefold, almost entirely in urban areas. As early as 1832, a doctor working in Manchester, J.P. Kay, graphically illustrated the key problems:

> The state of the streets powerfully affects the health of their inhabitants…Want of cleanliness, and of forethought are found in almost invariable alliance with dissipation, reckless habits and disease. The population gradually becomes physically less efficient as the producer of wealth… Were such manners to prevail, the horrors of pauperism would accumulate. A debilitated race would be rapidly multiplied. Morality would afford no check to the increase of population: crime and disease would be its only obstacles… They would drag on an unhappy existence, vibrating between the pangs of hunger and the delirium of dissipation – alternately exhausted by severe and oppressive toil, or enervated by supine sloth.

Clearly, a government that was evolving a far-reaching under-standing of its responsibility towards the people could not stand back and do nothing. Also, it was recognised that without state intervention to improve the situation, the whole economic miracle of the Industrial Revolution might collapse, as the ill health of the population affected its potential as a 'producer of wealth'. Also, increasing dissent amongst the workers posed another danger, as the revolutions that swept across Europe at the turn of the century had shown.

The first tentative steps toward a more interventionist state along these lines began even before Victoria came to the throne. The fear of the governing classes that the massively expanded proletariat might follow the example of half the nations of the continent had pushed the government to pass the 'Great' Reform Act of 1832, which slightly increased the size of the electorate. The following year came the first Factory Act, imposing a minimum set of working conditions for factories including the banning of the employment of young children and the provision that employers had to provide at least two hours of education a day for child employees and, perhaps more significantly, the Act also introduced the appointment of government inspectors to actually enforce the legislation. Once such measures were in place it had to be accepted that the improvement in conditions for those at the bottom of society had a positive effect on society as a whole, albeit modest.

Thus the Whigs, despite representing the landowning class, were keen to pursue further development of the state. In 1833, Parliament voted the first grant to support education for the poor. It was a paltry sum, which did not begin to provide for a system of state education, but it made provision for basic education to be provided by the Church and it was a precedent that set the path for increased investment throughout the nineteenth century culminating in the Education Act of 1870, which developed local board schools to complement the teaching of the Church. The Act was seen as a direct response to the expanded franchise of the 1867 Reform Act after which Robert Lowe, the Chancellor of the Exchequer said to the Prime Minister, William Gladstone: 'Now we must educate our masters!'

Compulsory elementary education followed in 1881 and the opportunity for almost all children to receive free elementary education without payment of any fees was provided by 1891. Responsibility for state-supported education was transferred, as Arthur Balfour put it, to 'those great public assemblies, the borough councils and the county councils of the country' in 1902. The setting up of a compulsory education system, even in such a tentative form, was a landmark in the development of the state's role in the life of the individual. Following Robert Peel's introduction of a police force, and the increased responsibility afforded to homeowners in the reforms of the 1830s, came the beginnings of a real relationship between the private and public sectors.

At these initial stages, that relationship was one that encouraged the freedom of the citizen, because the expanded franchise, safer streets, and a better educated population allowed each individual greater influence within a safer society. As the state develops, this must remain the standard by which further state intervention is measured. If it increases the freedoms of the people and improves their lives, it is acceptable. If, however, it merely imposes unnecessary restrictions on the lives of individuals, it is unacceptable.

The Great War, inevitably, plunged the country into a state of national emergency, and, as such, necessitated the restriction of personal freedoms in order to cope with it. But the Prime Minister, David Lloyd George, went as far as to declare in 1915 that the British people were '...fighting two great enemies, the Germans and drink'. This was a histrionic reference to the understandable habit of munitions workers having a few drinks after work, a practice which the government was convinced needed to be stamped out or, at least, firmly sat upon because of its effect on productivity.

King George V, a man not noted for legislative sophistication, had an idea. He invented The King's Pledge, proudly stating his intention not to touch another drop of alcohol until the Germans had been vanquished. It was his earnest belief that such a gesture would prove inspirational to his loyal subjects, who would instantly follow suit. That the Great War was psychically the greatest strain the nation had ever been under, and that its end was nowhere in sight, appeared not to affect his expectation that, in solidarity with their King, the people of Britain would give up their one source of pleasure and relief .

Lloyd George took a more practical approach by enforcing a temporary new law for the duration of the war forbidding public houses to stay open beyond eleven o'clock. That the measure was deemed necessary at a time when the nation was at war is perhaps understandable. That it is still in place eighty-six years later is not. It is possible that successive governments to that of Lloyd George have operated on the assumption that the Western Front is still at deadlock and that Kaiser Bill has not yet been persuaded to go home, but this is unlikely. What is more likely is that the trend of restrictive legislation is one that governments are reluctant to reverse.

New Labour have recently mooted proposals to relax the licensing laws, which would be an enlightened move were it instigated by a desire to expand people's freedoms. However, its motives for relaxing the laws are, ironically, much the same as those of Lloyd George for introducing them. While it was the habit of munitions workers to get 'a little tight' before bed that prompted Lloyd George to limit pubs' opening hours, it is the tendency of their descendants to get 'rat-arsed' before going to the disco that has prompted Blair to extend them. Blair has described 'binge drinking' as a 'new sort of British disease' whose cure, he hopes, will be found in banning 'Happy Hours' and keeping pubs open longer so that drinkers don't race to the bar to get their last five pints in before the eleven o'clock deadline.

It is worth noting that Churchill dismissed the King's Pledge at the time as a 'wheeze', displaying a lack of support which greatly angered Lloyd George, who had had the patriotism to decant all his gin into mineral water bottles for the sake of appearances. Indeed, the government in general appeared to think itself exempt from its own scheme, so much so that Churchill made a point of remarking on the marked diminution in energy and spirit of those, like Lord Birkenhead, who had taken the pledge: 'F.E. dined last night. Only cider and ginger pop! Rather morose – terrible results of intemperate self-restraint!'

Churchill's lofty contempt for such ruses as the King's Pledge conceals his deeper suspicion of the effects of too much state intervention. He was particularly disturbed by the revolution in Russia in 1917 and the rise of Bolshevism. He regarded the new Russian regime as not just a disaster for Russia but a menace to the whole world, referring to it in his work *The World Crisis* as

> ...not a wounded Russia only, but a poisoned Russia,
> an infected Russia, a plague-bearing Russia; a Russia
> of armed hordes smiting not only with bayonet and

> with cannon, but accompanied and preceded by
> swarms of typhus-bearing vermin which slew the
> bodies of men, and political doctrines which
> destroyed the health and even the soul of nations.

He also equated, slightly hysterically, Bolshevik tyranny with the Socialist movement in Britain and, in particular, the Labour Party, which had been founded by Keir Hardie in 1900 and had successfully presented itself as the true party of the working man. This was not terribly difficult at the beginning of the century, given that the Conservative administration was passing laws such as the Taff Vale judgment, whereby striking workers had to reimburse their employers for lost revenue if they went on strike. Vowing to overturn such policies saw 29 Labour MPs into Parliament in 1906, although Clement Attlee insisted that the party

> ...was not rigidly dogmatic, and preached a socialism
> which owed far more to the Bible than to Karl Marx. It
> was a characteristically British interpretation of
> socialism, a way of life rather than an economic dogma.

Whether characterised as a religious or a political doctrine, socialism naturally promotes an environment in which the state can meddle in the life of the individual, however 'British' Attlee claimed his interpretation was. Socialism in any form is a necessary precondition for the development of a controlling 'Nanny' state.

It was precisely this that worried the laissez-faire core of political thinkers in England, because a party describing itself as 'a way of life' sounded worryingly controlling. There was also something mildly creepy about the evangelical 'socialist movement' – Attlee fondly reminisced in his autobiography that '...this position of being a small fighting minority gave one a certain sense of exaltation. The capitalist fortress looked very strong and formidable and our forces were weak. We were crusaders in enemy-occupied territory...' Furthermore, in his history *The Labour Party in Perspective* in 1937 Attlee claimed '...to show the Labour Party in its historical setting as an expression in place and time of the urge for socialism, to show it as a characteristic example of British methods and as an outcome of British political instincts...'

The development of the Labour party and its 'characteristically British' interpretation of socialism bore little resemblance to Churchill's depiction of it as a 'menace'. After the Allied victory in 1945, his coalition government was replaced with a clear majority by a Labour government with Attlee at the helm. While his government's pursuit, in the name of socialism, of the nationalisation of industry did much, when he was in power, to damage British industry the two landmark achievements of his administration – the establishment of the Welfare State and the introduction of the NHS – can only be viewed as examples of enormous progress. The danger, however, is one which lurks within any enterprise wholly managed by the state; that of its exploitation by those who can see a means to get a share of the country's tax revenue, providing they can fool the state into believing that their services are necessary.

The 'peaceful revolution' brought about by the development of the social services seemed like a new dawn in post-war Britain. In 1951, with the economy in a mess, the Conservatives' first action on winning the election was to de-nationalise iron and steel and road transport. This set in motion a see-saw of socialist and conservative disagreement which would destabilise the economy for a generation. Attlee was hypocritical but accurate when he observed in 1954 that '...I think there is a danger here for the stability of the country, especially when the reversal is not based on national needs but merely on the ideological prejudices of a Party.'

He was referring to Conservative economic policy, but his words are an extremely eloquent summary of the democratic objection to the principle of a Nanny State. The vast expansion of social services has not stopped at the National Health or Unemployment Benefits or at any other logical, socially responsible point. It was bound to grow endlessly precisely because it was not founded solely on 'national needs' but on 'the ideological prejudices of a Party'.

The fact that Churchill's subsequent government kept hold of both the Welfare State and the NHS demonstrate that it is possible for one party to recognise that measures introduced by another can be effective and needn't necessarily be overturned because of ideological prejudice. The fact that all successive administrations to that of Attlee have seen the NHS in particular as something essential to the nation is testament to this.

The introduction of the NHS and the Welfare system are examples of the positive benefits of an expanded state, and their existence can only improve the life of the individual and, as with the introduction of schooling and a police force, further promote freedom – this time in the form of freedom from illness, or freedom from the purgatory of disability or unemployment. Where this can turn against the interests of the public is when such welfare policies are used by a government for electoral leverage. Blair and New Labour have seized control of the institutions of National Health and Welfare and used them as bargaining chips with the public. Smoking, obesity and excessive alcohol consumption are therefore clamped down on with the excuse of their alleged cost to the National Health Service, and a welfare system from which almost half the country are entitled to a payout is used as a means to secure its support.

The administration of Harold Wilson, beginning in 1963, was characterised by him as burning with 'the white heat of technology' Alongside the advancement of technology came the increased liberalisation of attitudes, especially among idealistic youth. While, overall, this liberalisation had many benefits to society, it also provided a vague ideology for the incubating officers of the Nanny State to hide behind. The alleged pursuit of a more 'liberal' society is often the excuse used by the present administration to impose more regulations. Ironically, the liberal outlook of the sixties has been blamed by Blair for the current increase in crime. On 19 July, 2004, he had the dishonesty to claim that, when he was young, 'people still left their doors unlocked', and that the hippy idealism of the Wilson years meant that people abandoned their respect for social responsibility. 'In the here and now,' he concluded, 'people have had enough of this part of the 1960s' consensus.'

However, for all Blair's disingenuousness, it is too late. The Sixties and the Seventies allowed for a small but self-propagating movement to develop. Under the banner of socialism, but armed with the new principles of 'equality' and 'welfare', a nannying agenda has been formed. One eye of its proponents has always been on the image of wishing to 'help' people, but the other has always been on the huge pile of cash that sits in the accounts of the Exchequer.

Under Thatcher, whose pursuit of a small state, an 'enterprise culture' and the privatisation of industry, there was little chance for these modern busybodies to find employment. However, in 1997, with Blair's achievement of balancing a capitalist economy with a socialist public life, there was an opening for those with a particular 'agenda' or 'issue' to rush in and grab a portion of the state's income. As a result the Nanny State is almost a direct product of the mystical 'Third Way', and is a symptom of one of that ideology's shortcomings.

It has taken Britain centuries to discover that the most effective state is a small one which helps the vulnerable and promotes freedom. The Nanny State is expensive, helps nobody and hinders freedom. Were Dickens writing in the twenty-first rather than the nineteenth century, the character Podsnap would doubtless still snort the same criticism as in *Our Mutual Friend*. No. Never with my consent. Not English.

2 If at first you don't succeed...

The Third Way - a clear, coherent route between the Right
...and the old, neo-Marxist Left.

Jack Straw, 1998

I want to lay to rest some of the myths around the Third Way. It is
not a third way between conservative and social democratic
philosophy.

Tony Blair, 2001

O n 1 May 1997, with the confident twitch of a deep red tie, two millennia of British history were suddenly deemed irrelevant. Tony Blair, 42, a public school educated barrister, swept into Downing Street with a massive majority, becoming the century's fourth 'socialist' prime-minister. 'This is a young country, a growing country,' he said, before attempting to validate this extraordinary statement by listing the ancient institutions that his government proposed to abolish.

'Things can only get better!' screamed the party's anthem, sung by the middle-aged 'pop' group D:Ream, and for a few weeks the nation was swept up in the excitement of its likable young prime minister and his fawning followers, who seemed prepared to sacrifice most of their values and all of their dignity in return for a break from eighteen long years in the political wilderness.

So excited were grassroots Labour supporters to have reclaimed the power they believed was rightfully theirs that most didn't waste any time reflecting on how exactly the victory had been achieved. One thing that had *not* been achieved was the triumph of socialist values over free-market capitalism, and while the architects of New Labour had embraced Tory economics, they had been guarded in admitting as much to the party faithful. They arrogantly assumed, too, that the sweet taste of victory would blind supporters to the uprooting of Labour's original values.

The first sign that Blair was determined to rid the party of its socialist heritage was evident as early as 1996. He shocked delegates at the annual party convention by proposing to rewrite Labour's 77-year-old charter, removing its almost sacred Clause Four, which declared the party's commitment to state-owned industry. The clause mandated that Labour should aim 'to secure for the workers...common ownership of the means of production, distribution and exchange'.

Blair's efforts had been opposed by trade-union members and the party's old guard, who sought to re-nationalise the industries that had been privatised during the 16-year reign of the Conservative Party. Throughout 1995, Blair conducted a national grassroots campaign to win the support of the party's constituents for his new Clause Four, insisting that Labour could only win the next election if it supported partial privatisation and embraced free-market ideals. Much to the fury of the trade unions, the new charter extolled the virtues of 'a dynamic economy [in which] the enterprise of the market and the rigour of competition are joined with the forces of partnership and cooperation...with a thriving private sector and high quality public services'.

Such a blatant retraction of one of the party's fundamental socialist principles damaged Blair's standing with the more militant wing. Without the retraction, however, Labour would have continued to be unelectable. Equally, without the backing of big business, Labour would not have been able to fight the election with the strength it did.

The extent of Blair's embrace of the business world was revealed almost immediately he entered Downing Street. In the first of a string of scandals it was revealed that New Labour had accepted a million pound 'donation' from Bernie Ecclestone, the dwarfish head of Formula One. In return, Labour reneged on its pledge to impose a blanket ban on tobacco advertising. Instead, it was allowed only where it turned a profit for the party's latest benefactor. Labour's persistent allegations of the Tory party being in the 'pockets of big business' were beginning to look a little hypocritical. Those who dreamed of an end to the destructive influence of multinational corporations and globalising industries were rapidly disillusioned. 'New' Labour were perceived as the ally of the corporate culture that had been so demonised under Thatcher, and donations from business amounted to over a third of Labour's total warchest, for the first time eclipsing donations from the trade unions. Blair's hypocrisy was also demonstrated by his changing attitude to the supermarket chain, Sainsbury's.

When Blair entered parliament in 1983, he was noted for his commitment to both unilateral nuclear disarmament and withdrawal from the European Community. Indeed, in an article for the *London Review of Books* in 1987 he criticised David Owen's Social Democratic Party for its rejection of both these principles, joking that because of its reliance on financial backing from the retail tycoon David Sainsbury the SDP was 'being relaunched as the political wing of Sainsbury's'.

This 'joke' has an awkward resonance now. While Blair has not (yet) dropped the bomb on another sovereign nation nor (yet) engineered total British integration into Europe, snide jokes about accepting support from business, and Sainsbury's in particular, would now seem extraordinarily inappropriate. If Blair could describe the SDP as the 'political wing' of Sainsbury's seventeen years ago, perhaps he would concede that his party now houses the supermarket's combined meat, fish, frozen foods, and hosiery departments. In 1996-7 alone Sainsbury donated £3 million to the party, with further donations bringing the total to £7 million in just five years.

Such generosity, of course, did not go unrecognised. Sainsbury received his seat in the House of Lords in 1998, and a ministerial post the following year. While parliamentary etiquette demanded the new

Lord Sainsbury's resignation as chairman of the board of Sainsbury's, the company seemed to actively benefit from the loss. In 1998, planning permission was mysteriously granted to the chain's new out-of-town supermarkets, despite the initial refusal of local councils. The controversy surrounding the new 'Minister for Science' escalated when he was reported to have loaned Diatech, a member of the BioIndustry Association, money to buy a £2 million office in Westminster a mere eight days before taking up his appointment.

Blair had accepted Thatcher's view and embraced the 'Enterprise Culture' himself. It seemed likely that he would now reject big government and the intrusion of the Nanny State. However, part of his political brilliance is his ability to be all things to all people, and he managed to dream up a compromise. New Labour intended to show that it was possible to pursue a proto-socialist program of interference in public life whilst maintaining a 'dynamic enterprise culture'.

For an ostensibly socialist government to justify its reliance on big-business for donations, and be prepared for the same businesses to then dictate the running of the economy, might seem paradoxical. However, such a paradox was easily reconciled by means of the elusive 'Third Way'. This apparently revolutionary development in political philosophy is notoriously difficult to understand – so much so that none of its main proponents seem able to agree on what exactly it is or, when they do agree, to explain it to anybody else.

It was originally the brainchild of Professor Anthony Giddens, whose book *The Third Way* (1998) was a means to justify his own drift from the left to the right, whilst pretending that such a drift had never taken place. Its desperate bid to convince not just its audience of its credibility but also its own author is evident on every page. It claims to offer a new political philosophy that 'goes beyond right and left'. What it really offers is a rather feeble compromise. But as centrist governments across the world were all looking at the time for just such a compromise, he hit a rich vein of support. It was insisted that Giddens' big idea was not a 'compromise' but a 'new way', and lofty concepts such as going 'beyond' what had come before and the new 'way ahead' litter its exposition.

Giddens' ambitious attempt to reconcile irreconcilable ideas continues in *The Third Way and Its Critics* (2000), which is in favour of the deregulation of companies. Whilst he admits that 'flexibility does indeed entail deregulation' he also feels that deregulated corporations such as Microsoft are an evil that 'left-of-centre governments mustn't shirk confronting'. Giddens' rather touching desire to be all things to all people naturally touched a nerve in the equally keen-to-please Tony Blair, who seized on it with almost the same religious fervour as Bill Clinton.

The President announced with great gravity in his 1998 State of the Union address: 'My fellow Americans, we have found a Third Way.' Lacking the lovable mixture of sexual indiscretion and pious self-belief that allowed his American counterpart to get away with such a Messianic pronouncement, Blair had to rely on his usual 'I'm an honest guy, me' approach to convince people that his latest wheeze had any substance.

The magic formula allowed the Nanny State to operate alongside a culture of enterprise. Previous socialist doctrine maintained that the individual could only be protected from greedy companies by the state. Taking direct control over industry and therefore protecting the citizen from its excesses at source was not the Third Way. For New Labour, the ill-effects of competitive capitalism can only be countered *after* they have taken place. Therefore the current government effectively allows business to operate unchecked, and then steps in with ineffective legislation to protect the citizen from the consequences.

The Third Way pleased those in the business community because it was ideologically it was no different than Thatcherism, but it also aimed to placate the idealists who still believed in the 'big state' philosophy of the old socialists. The Nanny State is a consequence of this, wielded by the latter to supposedly check the excesses of the former. The lunacy of a political philosophy that encourages a competitive economy and then punishes it with legislation and taxes is obvious. Its supporters tend to overlook the fact that society's ills are often caused by the same ideology that tries to cure them.

The Guardian carried a leader on New Year's Day 2004 entitled 'Britain needs the Nanny State now more than ever' in which the author, Jackie Ashley, painted a picture of a Britain in which:

> ...it is the poorer...who are most visibly damaged by the downside of consumerism. This is pretty simple. If you can't afford the expensive consolations of winter travel or dinners out, then the homelier treats of chocolate, burgers and alcopops are that much harder to resist. Fat now means poor. Pop Idol's 15-stone Michelle is a working-class girl

who stands, and wobbles, for millions. Pass a group of kids smoking and the odds are they will be female and poor. And if poorer families fall down on the parenting front, they can't buy in foreign girls to help plug the gaps.'

Phrases like 'visibly damaged' and 'the downside of consumerism' do their best to make the point seem worthwhile, but even a brief consideration of this sentence leads the reader to the less florid statement that 'Poor people are poor'. Even Ashley had the largesse to concede that 'this is pretty simple''. She accepts that those who cannot afford winter holidays and dining out are likely to find "the homelier treats of chocolate, burgers and alcopops are that much harder to resist'. The connection between skiing and not wanting to eat chocolate is tenuous at best, but for Ashley trips to Meribel and Nobu and drinking alcopops are mutually exclusive. It also carries with it the horribly patronising implication that poor people only have Whoppers and Smirnoff Ices to alleviate the pain of their existence.

She concludes, however, that the Nanny State is the only viable way to help the vulnerable in such a world. Like many of the Nanny State's supporters she assumes that the 'whole point' of progressive politics 'is to stand with the most vulnerable people'. Which translates as attacking 'the great commercial, short-termist forces' that have made them that way. One would hope that the 'whole point' of progressive politics is greater than to 'stand with the vulnerable'. Some might argue that the 'whole point' of progressive politics is to stop the 'vulnerable' being so by providing them with a decent education and a responsible state that counters these exploitive commercial forces at root, rather than offering belated apologies to the vulnerable for allowing and, in many cases, encouraging their existence in the first place.

A responsible state should provide the vulnerable with sufficient education to enable them to make informed choices, then should create an employment market that enables the poor to bring themselves out of poverty. Instead, the employment market is reaching saturation point with vacancies for the meddling and otherwise unemployable enforcers of the Nanny State, all of whom are desperate to peddle their own particular brand of cultural and social totalitarianism. Neatly, most of their individual obsessions are catered for under the catch-all banner of Third Way progressive politics.

The logic of allowing competition to drive the economy, with all its inevitable problems, and then introducing legislation to protect the public from themselves, is the politics of doublethink. It makes absolute sense to the architects of the Nanny State, however, prominent amongst whom is Professor John Ashton, the 'Regional Director of Public Health for the North West, who in 2003 spelt out the Nanny State's mission statement:

> Individuals cannot protect themselves from bio-terrorism, epidemics of Sars, the concerted efforts of the junk food industry, drug dealers and promoters of tobacco and alcohol.... A civilised society will provide a legislative framework to protect people, and in particular the most vulnerable. Criticism of the nanny state is almost always misplaced and is frequently nonsensical. The State is the

guardian of the weak and underprivileged...it has a duty to
ensure that those less well-off in society have safe, warm,
low-cost housing, convenient transport links to shops and
amenities, and the protection of police on the streets.

A civilised society clearly has a duty to protect its most
vulnerable, and to provide an infrastructure within which they can
operate, but these structures should promote freedom, not inhibit it.
The purpose of a country's legislation, and of the law, is to enable its
citizens to move about unhindered by other people, and protected
from the tyranny of monopolies. However, beyond that, a civilised
society should allow its citizens to make informed and responsible
decisions, not have the legislature make such decisions for them.

Professor Ashton's defiant assertion that individuals in general
'*cannot protect themselves*' demonstrates the kind of patronising,
defeatist thinking that underpins the Nanny State. Human beings have
perfectly happily been protecting themselves for hundreds of
thousands of years from far greater perils than the 'concerted efforts
of the junk food industry' and have battled through to tell the tale. The
idea that suddenly they should have to abandon their resilience and
seek refuge in the arms of the state is condescending in the extreme.
It fosters the absurd modern idea that man is essentially a doomed
creature, incapable of independent thought, and totally ill-equipped to
survive in this hostile environment. He cannot hope to survive, that
is, unless he is surrounded by legions of fawning counsellors and
social workers translating his problems into meaningless
psychobabble. Then they diagnose him with invented psychological
problems, invariably rooted in a sexually-abused childhood, and then

protect him from himself with sufficient legislation to render autonomous decisions impossible. The Nanny State refuses to concede that people may, in fact, be the authors of their own lives.

Professor Ashton also believes that the only practical way to contain the recent increase in sexually transmitted diseases is for the government to take control of illegal brothels and make sure that they are subject to 'rigorous registration, regulation, and inspection...like there is in abattoirs'. Aside from the almost poetic imagery of Ashton's comparison of sex and execution , his suggestion shows how intimate the State's relationship with the citizen may soon become. Nanny will not just be defending her charges from the dangers of the nursery, but standing in the bedroom barking out instructions and advice as well.

For the Nanny State's agenda, one need look no further than the nursery of Professor Ashton's house. He recently had a child with his 'partner', Maggi Morris, a 'Director of Public Health' in Preston. The poor creature was named 'Fabian Che Jed', after the Fabian Society, Che Guevara and the prophet Jedediah. Ignoring, for the time being, the psychological trauma that the child is doubtless going to suffer in the playground for his embarrassing name, and ignoring also the simple vulgarity of using an innocent child as a banner from which to hang one's political affiliations, it is worth considering what Fabian Che Jed symbolises about the new establishment.

His parents like to give the impression that they are the ideological descendants of the Marxists, groomed on the exciting but nowadays redundant language of the class warriors and hippy idealists of the polytechnics in the Sixties and Seventies. They are not, however, and their political pretensions are as patronising to those they claim to represent as they are repellent to those they claim to oppose. Their political hypocrisy is similar to that of Andy Gilchrist, the chief of the fire union, who has a large poster of Che Guevara behind his desk and constantly recommends that firefighters go on strike to demand more pay, while he happily draws his £82,000 a year salary and puts £800 dinners in the Cinnamon Club on his union's expense account.

Finding their cause somewhat emasculated by the country's economic revival during the last quarter of the century, the new breed of middle-class 'social warriors' have had to abandon the more ambitious aspects of their social projects and restrict themselves to fiddling on the periphery. With the genuine horrors of cholera, large-scale poverty and injustice largely eradicated in this country, they instead go about finding themselves things to do to protect the 'vulnerable' from the more innocuous dangers of capitalist excess. It is symptomatic of the dearth of serious issues that their concerns have had to become ever more ridiculous, tackling 'stress' problems or 'bullying in the workplace'. Having exhausted the patience of free-thinking adults with such patronising rubbish, the meddling do-gooders have extended their concern to 'victims' that cannot tell them to go away, like children, animals, and bewildered immigrants.

The gobbledegook language of Marxism found its true heir in the gobbledegook language of postmodernism, a new intellectual basis for the left's totalitarian aspirations. 'Intellectual' is perhaps a generous term, because one of postmodernism's defining features is that it feeds on a side-stepping of rigorous analysis and logical thought. For a generation of those who felt alienated by the strict methodology of 'conventional' academia it was a godsend. Why waste years of one's life coming to terms with the complicated and intellectually demanding language and concepts of real branches of science, when one could immediately gain respect without having to do any proper work? That was itself a very postmodern concept. It lent itself to a passionate protection of 'minorities' as well.

To a postmodernist, what we believe to be true in the West is merely subjective truth. Our 'science' is no more valid a discipline than the East's mysticism or the pagan belief in the deity of trees. As with the child pointing out that the emperor wasn't wearing any clothes, such ideas gained an enormous following before anybody dared to point out that they were all humbug. If scientific reasoning and discovery is only subjectively true, then it would follow that those cultures whose world view cannot accommodate it cannot benefit from it. Therefore medicine would have no effect on Aborigines, the telephone would not function if used by New Age Travellers, and aeroplanes would not even take off with Islamic Fundamentalists at the controls.

Tom Wolfe, in his essay 'Hooking Up', sent-up the post-modern 'deconstructionists' who supposedly 'deconstruct' the truth:

> Oddly, when deconstructionists required appendectomies or bypass surgery or even a root-canal job, they never deconstructed medical or dental 'truth', but went along with their board-certified, profit-oriented surgeons proclaimed was the last word.

The postmodernists ignored such lampooning and the movement continued almost religiously. Absolutely incompatible cultures and religions were reasoned to be 'equally valid', language was seen to be a mechanism of slavery, and the 'rights' of minorities were elevated above those of the majority.

The logic bore a frightening resemblance to that of O'Brien, the torturer in *Nineteen Eighty-Four*, who lectures the man he is torturing:

> You believe that reality is something objective, external, existing in its own right.... But I tell you, Winston, that reality is not external. Reality exists in the human mind, and nowhere else. Not in the individual mind, which can make mistakes, and in any case soon perishes: only in the mind of the Party, which is collective and immortal. Whatever the Party holds to be truth, *is* truth.

Under the banner of postmodernism, encouraged by the embrace of the magical Third Way, a number of exciting new projects were given the green light. They merely required legislative coercion rather than any logical acceptance. Prominent among these was the quest for 'Political Correctness' which now hampers every aspect of modern life, despite being laughed at by the majority of the population.

The phrase was coined by the Russian Communist Party in the 1930s and seized on by students in American and English Campuses in the late Eighties and early Nineties. 'Hey, Hey, Ho, Ho, Western Culture's Got to Go' chanted students at Stanford University in 1988, supported in person by Rev. Jesse Jackson. Their demand, echoed by left-wing students across the globe, was that readings of 'DWEMs' ('Dead White European Male' writers) be replaced by supposedly more relevant female, homosexual and Third World authors.

Shakespeare was taught, not to entertain, inform, or inspire, but 'to illuminate the way seventeenth-century society mistreated women, the working class, and minorities'. With great excitement, the left got to work on dreaming up all sorts of schemes to liberate the beleaguered minorities, without beginning to worry about how patronising they were actually being. The fact that the twentieth century had seen such a horrific history of intolerance, prejudice and oppression provided ammunition for their ideas, and a convenient rebuttal to anyone who argued with their philosophy. Branding anybody who refuses to concede to their every argument a 'Nazi' may be crass and insensitive, but it works. The liberal left have been utilising this vacuous and arrogant strategy since the politically correct movement began. So entrenched have the ideas of political correctness become that they have succeeded in destabilising the very semantics of our language. Witness the ludicrous attempt to take the alleged 'sexism' out of English, with perfectly innocuous words like 'manager', 'chairman' and 'mankind' being deemed insulting. Once established, the 'racism', 'sexualism', 'ageism', and even the 'disablism' bandwagons all thundered along in sexism's wake. The greatest indecency in the movement is that it is so *unnecessary*. The emancipation of women, the civil rights movements in America, the widespread adoption of liberal values, and mass immigration have meant that many of the old social hierarchies have been stripped away and a new awareness of prejudice and inequality has come to be appreciated by society anyway. The liberalisation of attitudes has developed naturally without the counter-productive meddling of the left.

The postmodern thought process allows practitioners to alter definitions of words as they see fit. A favourite exercise is to abandon the notion that anything can be described as what it *is*, but only as what it is *not*. Grafting definitions onto ideas, philosophies, or peoples, is supposedly an attempt at enslaving them. Such lofty nonsense is directly behind the attempts of this much derided lobby to redefine anything that relates to a perceived 'minority'. Thus, those who used to be blind are now 'visually impaired', those who used to be black are now 'not-white' or 'of colour' and those who once thought of themselves as 'disabled' are now 'differently able.' Pointless as these re-definitions are, and unfashionable as they are fast becoming, the main objection to them is how blatantly *offensive* they are to those that they refer. To describe a Negro as black is as valid as it is to describe a Caucasian as white. To refer to a Negro as 'not-white', however, is implicitly to suggest that there is something wrong with him. As much as to say that he is 'off-white' or 'dirty'.

In America, the National Federation of the Blind were so fed up with the absurd euphemisms used to describe its members (including a Congress-issued directive to educational establishments that the blind were to be described as 'persons of visual impairment or diminution') that they petitioned the government, declaring that:

> We believe that it is respectable to be blind, and although
> we have no particular pride in the fact of our blindness,

neither do we have any shame in it. To the extent that euphemisms are used to convey any other concept or image, we deplore such use. We can make our own way in the world on equal terms with others, and we intend to do it.

Sadly, such outbursts of indignant common sense are rare, and more often than not the dignity of minorities is ignored as the politically correct lobby march about campaigning on their behalf.

One of the most appalling aspects of the movement is the idea that social cachet can be attached to the rejection of prejudice. The fact is that prejudices such as racism should be rejected because they are wrong, ignorant and divisive, not because because some pop star or football player has said that it is 'cool' to do so. This is the problem with movements like 'Rock against Racism' and 'Give Racism the Red Card'; although they are clearly founded with the best intentions, they are worrying because they rely on their message being fashionable and trendy. Fashion, especially in the teen world that these campaigns aim to influence, continually changes, so to try to lump anti-racism in with the latest Nike trainers is mad, as it presumably accepts that 'anti-racism' will be in the dustbin alongside the trainers come next spring. The apparently ephemeral nature of anti-racism was most absurdly highlighted by the European Union's designation of 1997 as the 'European Year Against Racism'. On New Year's Day, 1998, it was apparently alright for people across Europe to start discriminating again.

Perhaps the most cringe-worthy display of this viciously misguided aspect of political correctness came in April 2004, with the now notorious rap song performed by North Wales' deputy Chief

Constable, Clive Wolfendale, at the inaugural meeting of the North Wales Black Police Association.

DCC Wolfendale, is middle-aged, middle-class, very white, and has silver hair. The following are extracts from his 'song':

> I'm just a white boy called the Deputy CC
> They said I'd never make it as a bitchin' MC
>
> So listen! Watch a doin' here today
> Checkin' what the Heddlu Gogledd Cymru gotta say
>
> Bein' in the dibble is no cakewalk when you're black
> If you don't get fitted, then you'll prob'ly get the sack
>
> Job ain't what it used to be; it's full of blacks and gays
> It was just us white homies in the really good ole' days
>
> The BPA is sayin' that we're all in the same boat
> Black or white in blue, we're all wearin' the same coat
>
> So Roger, Nick and Larbi will you give us one more chance
> Danny and Silvana, I'd really like to dance
>
> Thank you all for coming and remember what we say
> Support your local sheriff and the North Wales BPA.

The outrage caused by the 'rap' was universal, with the chairman of the Commission for Racial Equality, Trevor Phillips, saying, 'Presumably this was an attempt to get down with their supposed culture. How wrong. How patronising. How demeaning.'

DCC Wolfendale's response to Phillips was simple, 'Without wishing to sound patronising,' he replied, 'I think Mr Phillips has missed the point.' Whether or not Mr. Phillips did miss the point, it seems that the audience of his rap did not. 'As far as I understand, the majority of officers that were present were offended by it,' said North Wales Black Police Association spokesman, Clive Morris.

No doubt they are also offended by the Nanny State's attitude towards multiculturalism. The central ideal of multiculturalism is rooted in postmodernism. All cultures and means of looking at the world are equally valid, so it is wrong to promote one above another, runs the argument. Therefore, immigrants to this country should not be expected to conform to its values, and are instead encouraged to live here as they would have done at home. For this apparently divisive strategy to work the government believes it just needs to promote 'equality', 'understanding' and 'tolerance.' The result is further inequality, prejudice and intolerance, but this is overlooked by the crusading multiculturalists.

The government-sponsored website 'Britkid' is a no doubt well-intentioned initiative to encourage children to embrace the ideal of multiculturalism. Its agenda is made very clear on its homepage, where a group of eight children (John, Megan, Nat Mumtaz, David, Bal, Anand, Dani and Tzu-Lee) are depicted in suitably demure poses. Only two of them are white (John and David), and David turns out to be a Scottish Jew. The 'gang' live in the mythical town of Britchester where they hang out in places like the Burger Bar, the Sports Stadium, Pete's Pizza and the Gurudwara.

In each place visitors to the site can 'listen' to the conversations the Britkids have with each other, so in the 'ICT Suite' we hear a conversation between Tzu-Lee, John, and David about David's

Judaism – a conversation instigated by Tzu-Lee calling David a 'Jew' because he refuses to give her one of his crisps. The conversation continues to discuss anti-semitism and other forms of racial prejudice. At one point the British treatment of the Chinese in Hong-Kong is compared to the Nazis' treatment of the Jews.

In another area of Britchester, 'Glitz' clothing, we witness the following discussion that takes place amongst the clothing rails:

Megan (Black African): So look, shall I buy this top or not?

Dani (Black Carribean): In what colour?

Megan: Oh I dunno. I can't decide...

Anand (Indian): Well, I vote for blue. It goes well with your skin colour.

Tzu Lee (Chinese): Coloured? Who - what?

Anand: No, I didn't say -

Tzu Lee: I mean, what is 'coloured' anyway? It's sort of ducking the issue isn't it? I mean, we're not green or red are we...

There then follows a long argument about the difference between each skin colour, at which the young (black) shop assistant intervenes by telling Megan, 'You're not getting any whiter!' The conversation concludes simply with Megan saying, 'I'm confused!'

For that, at least, Megan cannot be blamed. The site's overall aim is to clear up the confusion caused by multiculturalism, but by constantly stressing the differences between each member of 'the gang', it prevents the members having much in common. It goes to great lengths to stress the equal validity of each of the Britkids' cultures and religions. At one point, in an article about

'Islamophobia', it argues that the fundamentalists' hatred of the West should be interpreted as 'perhaps having a view on life and the world worth listening to'. Furthermore, where Islam is criticised for its treatment of women and young people it should instead be praised for 'having strong moral standards'.

One thing that the website never does is allow any of the various-hued 'Brit Kids' to identify themselves as having a culture in common. Instead, they are supposedly united through their diversity. It is this aspect of multiculturalism, more than its sheer condescension, that is the most dangerous.

The ludicrous leader of the British National Party, Nick Griffin, was once asked what his party meant by 'British'. He replied as follows:

> We mean the bonds of culture, race, identity and roots of the native British peoples of the British Isles. We have lived in these islands near on 40,000 years! We were made by these islands, and these islands are our home. When we in the BNP talk about being British, we talk about the native peoples who have lived in these islands since before the Stone Age.

While many of the views of Griffin's party can draw comparisons with the Stone Age, how its members can possibly claim such a pure pedigree is a mystery.

Part of England's historical success has always been that she is a nation of immigrants. From the Vikings, through the Romans, the Norman Conquest and the subsequent millennium of immigration of people from the far reaches of the empire, and those granted refugee status by successive sympathetic governments, Britain has always been a nation defined by the different people that have come to live here. Contrary to Nick Griffin and the vile claim of the British Nationalist Party that immigration is an evil that presents a threat to the British way of life, it is actually as central a part of Britain's development as the discovery of tea or the clarification of the Oxford Laws of Croquet. Immigrants used to be absorbed without ceremony, but now, under the influence of postmodernism, they are no longer expected by the government to conform to the British mode of living. They are encouraged to live here exactly as they did at home, rejecting accepted cultural standards whilst taking the benefits living in this country brings with it. The immigrant population can hardly be blamed for taking advantage of this, but it puts the state in a bizarre position. Such is its tolerance that it must welcome those who show it intolerance. We welcome cultures whose attitudes towards, for example, women, children, or animals, we consider abhorrent, encouraging them to continue as they always have done out of respect for their 'culture'.

This is not just hypocritical but also irresponsible, racist, and inevitably divisive. To encourage immigrants to reject British culture – especially in those cases where it has been the very intolerance of their own countries that has compelled them to seek refuge in ours – must be destructive. Such groups want to preserve their own way of life, doubtless in the hope that, when their own country becomes more democratic or just 'tolerant', they will return. Unfortunately, the latter rarely happens. Meanwhile, they build up resentment at their differences with their, supposedly, temporary host culture.

Britain should be proud to welcome people from all over the world, and keen to learn what it can from them, but never at the expense of our culture. The latter has developed in a way that has at its heart the very tolerance that attracts such immigrants. As it stands, multiculturalism is divisive. No effort is asked of immigrant populations to integrate, and they are effectively ghettoised into their own communities. The inevitable feeling of alienation, especially amongst the young, who often feel that they have their feet in two entirely different worlds, leads to social apartheid that in turn breeds a culture of disaffection from which the imams of *jihad* can and do recruit 'martyrs'.

This is not to suggest that immigrants should abandon their ancient traditions and beliefs in order to come and live here. Where those traditions and beliefs do not fit, however, they must necessarily adapt. Generally, the people that understand this the best are the immigrants themselves, as the extraordinarily vibrant melting pot of cultures that happily co-exist in parts of London and other big cities demonstrate. Yet, they have achieved this despite, rather than because of, the efforts of nannying social workers. They have not been helped by the politically correct lobby trying to elevate the status of foreign cultures above the status of British culture. The ultimate aim of immigration should be that those who come to live in England, for example, should feel proud to describe themselves as 'English' and consider the flag of their adopted country their own. The absurd rejection of all that should be best about immigration inevitably plays into the hands of racists such as the BNP. It is the concept of multiculturalism itself that does the most to promote racism and intolerance.

Trevor Phillips accepted this in a rejection of the multiculturalism in a speech to Black civil servants in April, 2004. The policies previously implemented were 'misguided' he claimed, and 'inherently racist.' Political correctness led to 'benign neglect' of ethnic minorities, and the emphasis on multiculturalism further alienated minorities.

He cited the case of social workers in Tottenham who failed to intervene in the case of Victoria Climbié, an eight-year-old girl from the Ivory Coast who died in 2000 after months of abuse, torture and neglect by her great aunt and her great aunt's boyfriend. The inquiry into Victoria's death established that the social workers believed the girl's fear of her great aunt was part of her African culture, which emphasised respect for elders. 'There is no aspect of African culture that demands that we turn a blind eye to the degradation and murder of a human being,' Mr Phillips noted. No doubt the social workers who stood back and did nothing thought they were merely witnessing a different 'culture' with equal validity to our own.

With this ideological confusion has come a re-definition of 'rights'. So great was the advancement in the quality of life in the latter half of the twentieth century that serious illness no longer confronts people as they walk down the street. Life has become a highly sanitised, sheltered and immunised affair, with death largely confined to (admittedly grossly understaffed) hospitals. Life, health and happiness, argue the new left, are not just the products of enormous good fortune, but 'rights' which it is the state's duty to protect. The idea that there should be an articulated set of human 'rights' is indicative of how civilised we have become. We aspire to live in a society where such rights are both protected and enforced, but no society can transcend human fallibility. If any of our human rights *are* violated, we are encouraged to feel that something has gone terribly wrong rather than that our world has fallen short of an aspirational state. We all know it is extremely damaging to expect life to be perfect, but our innate cultural common sense is being undermined by a government misguidedly legislating towards Utopia.

If Tony Blair has read *Utopia* he would know that Thomas More's original vision of the perfect society was ironic, filled with miserably lethargic Utopians. The unfeasibility of legislating towards the perfect state is captured by the very word Utopia, which derives equally from *eu topos*, the Greek for 'good place', and *ou topos*, the Greek for 'no place'. Thomas More's own government, however, rewarded him for his work by burning him at the stake and ours is doing pretty much the same thing to his philosophy.

Tony Blair has frequently espoused his belief that there 'cannot be rights without responsibilities'. Unfortunately, this has not stopped his government from attaching an almost sacred aspect to the notion of rights. Any legislation is deemed fit to pass if it claims to protect the 'rights' of something, be it the individual, the minority, the persecuted, or in the most extreme cases, defenceless animals.

The idea that animals should be granted 'rights' is meaningless. Since the animals themselves cannot be made aware of their rights the idea that they have 'rights' which must be protected means nothing to them, and is therefore entirely subjective. It is similar to the little girl who declares that Barbie is married to Ken. As far as she is concerned the two plastic figurines are married to each other, but it means nothing to the alleged 'husband' and 'wife', because they are made of plastic and cannot think.

Of course, no civilised human being wants to inflict any unnecessary harm on animals. Indeed, the cultures of all hunting societies are marked by the honour shown to the prey that sustains their way of life. This respect for other animals does get eroded in industrial societies and practices like the battery farming of chickens are disgusting and purely a means to maximise profit, without showing any concern for the creatures involved. The fact remains, however, that human beings *necessarily* rely on animals as a food source, and on their skins and furs for keeping warm. Provided that no unnecessary suffering is inflicted on the animals, such a practice is not merely perfectly acceptable, it is unalterably natural.

The argument about scientific experimentation is more complicated, but most animal-loving people would agree that it is better for scientists to experiment on rats and monkeys if the results of those experiments are going to find cures for human diseases and, in the process, end the need for animal testing. Animals' lives rarely end peacefully, however they die. Nature is perhaps the most ruthless culler of all, well beyond huntsmen, meat-eaters or research scientists. In the wild nothing dies in the comfort of its own bed, surrounded by loved ones and a photographic record of its memories,. Wild animals die at the claws of predators, ravaged by disease, of starvation from having lost the strength to hunt for food, or from exhaustion.

The extreme wing of the animal rights movement, however, refuses to think realistically. The People for the Ethical Treatment of Animals, or PETA, is to animal lovers what al-Quaeda is to Islam. They believe that all animals should be treated with exactly the same respect as humans. A crime against an animal should be punished in the same way as a crime against a human being.

One of their mantras is 'A rat is a pig is a dog is a boy', used to demonstrate their belief that the lives of each are of equal value. Many of them go further and with their acts of terrorism demonstrate their belief that the lives of animals are of greater value than those of humans. In a particularly spectacular display of mindless stupidity, the 'Animal Liberation Front' posted a site on the internet called 'Your Guide to Putting the Heat on Animal Abusers Everywhere', which explained to its would-be assassins how to target carnivores with arson attacks. As if the various groups were competing with each other to see which could come up with the vilest means of attention seeking, PETA responded by sending Armin Miewes, the German cannibal who admitted slaughtering, butchering and eating a man he met over the internet, a vegetarian cookbook and a hamper full of veggie burgers in the hope of converting him to vegetarianism. 'What this man did to a German computer expert is done to other creatures every day,' a PETA spokesman explained. 'The cruel scenario of slaughtering, cutting up, portioning, freezing and eating of body parts is the grim reality for more than 450 million sentient individuals that are killed in (Germany) every year.'

Such sentiments would be ridiculous enough if PETA had accurately represented the Miewes case, but their creative re-interpretation omitted the point that the victim had been a willing participant. The Miewes campaign doesn't even come close to the most depraved of PETA's strategies. In their campaign 'The Final Solution', they claimed that 'Like the Jews murdered in concentration camps, animals are terrorised when they are housed in huge filthy warehouses and rounded up for shipment to slaughter. The leather sofa and handbag are the moral equivalent of the lampshades made from the skins of people killed in the death camps.' In the wake of predictable outrage from Jewish groups, the organisation made the following statement:

> Decades from now, what will you tell your grandchildren when they ask you whose side you were on during the animals' holocaust? Will you be able to say that you stood up against oppression, even when doing so was considered "radical" or "unpopular"? Will you be able to say that you could visualize a world without violence and realized that it began at breakfast?

Groups like PETA and the ALF can easily be laughed off as the lunatic fringe, but already the influence of their thinking is showing through in the meddling of the Nanny State. After the Ecclestone debacle, it was widely reported that New Labour had accepted £1.1 million pounds worth of persuasive 'donations' from animal rights groups with links to the unhinged extreme. Sure enough, legislation to curb 'abuses' of animal rights was almost immediately proposed, beginning with the vitriolic campaign to ban fox-hunting.

Labour backbenchers have pursued the ban with surprising venom given that they are more than happy to allow the continued practice of Halal butchery and coarse fishing. For most of the party, the issue of fox-hunting has nothing whatsoever to do with the welfare of the fox, and everything to do with the pursuit of a 'grand gesture'. All the old, and now largely redundant class hatreds and insecurities of the socialists come into play with the issue and, for Blair, the tiny minority that pursues hunting is a safe enemy to make, compared to the large numbers of voters that eat Halal meat or enjoy torturing unlovable fish for sport.

Oscar Wilde's opinion of fox-hunting as the 'unspeakable in pursuit of the inedible' is an entirely subjective one, perfectly reasonable for an individual to hold but not one that should be assumed by a government as part of its legislative remit. On almost every ideological count, a ban on hunting fails in its professed intention.

First, the majority of hunt supporters are not the 'toffs' that the brutish anti hunt brigade delight in portraying them. Most are country people on the low income afforded them by the government-ruined farming industry.

Second, given that the issue is being fought under the pretence of an animal rights agenda, the banning of hunting can only, ultimately, increase the suffering of animals. The enormous number of horses and hounds that are used in hunting have not been trained for any other purpose and, in the event of a ban, will have to be put down. Also, the fox, which is one of the few animals in the wild that hunts and kills with indifference, will be given free rein to scavenge around the place killing as it pleases. The animal rights groups have not yet suggested that animals should be given the vote, but it can only be a matter of time, and when ducks and chickens do receive the franchise – and they will far outnumber foxes – it will be interesting to see whether or not they vote in favour of re-introducing hunting.

Ducks and chickens, along with creatures even further down the evolutionary chain, while perhaps feeling persecuted by the government's championing of their natural enemy, may take some solace in the amended Animal Rights Act of 1911. Pushed for by the RSPCA, which has increasingly drifted in the direction of the fanatics, a draft version was presented to parliament by the animal health and welfare minister, Ben Bradshaw, on 14 July 2004. The act specifically demands a 'duty of care' for all persons in charge or in control of an animal, and provides for an offence of 'likely to cause unnecessary suffering'. This would all seem perfectly reasonable, except that supporters of the act require that the 'duty of care' includes requirements to 'attend to the psychological needs of an animal', which in practice means anthromorphising animals to an absurd degree. There is even a suggestion that, should scientists be able to prove that molluscs can experience pain and suffering, accidentally treading on a snail could become a criminal offence. John Cushnie, panellist on BBC Radio 4's *Gardener's Question Time*, expressed his outrage to the *Daily Telegraph*:

> To give worms and slugs protection under the law is ludicrous. If I have an infestation of slugs or snails or cabbage white butterflies then I will get rid of them in whatever way I choose. No one is going to tell me that the

things are suffering. If I want to boil them alive, stamp on them or treat them to a slow drawn-out death by poison then I will – and I would like to see the government that would try to interfere with a man and his garden.

In June 2004, the RSPCA signed a written agreement with the secretary of state for environment, food and rural affairs, to allow it to perform the function of an 'approved prosecutor'. This will come into effect on 1 September 2004, and will effectively grant the RSPCA greater powers than the police. The RSPCA, however, has gradually been becoming a wilfully incompetent and fanatical body, who will suddenly be given powers to prosecute whosoever they please, and will be answerable to no one.

From this it can be seen how the Nanny State has come into existence. It harbours socialist pretensions but ultimately is not prepared to go the whole way; equally it preys on a capitalist economy while claiming to despise capitalism. The 'Third Way' and the various attractive-sounding philosophies that New Labour offered provided a Trojan Horse for the Nanny State to hide within during the 1997 election, only to sneak out and start pursuing its own agenda once its parent was in power. Perhaps a better analogy would be that of the computer virus which hides in a pleasant sounding email. 'Lovely Topless Girls!' claims the subject line of the spam, only, once it has been opened, to release a hard-drive destroying 'worm'.

New Labour made all sorts of exciting promises to the country while in opposition: an end to political corruption, better education, less crime, and so on. Once in power, however, all it seemed to offer was widespread evidence of its own corruption accompanied by armies of frantically busy 'officers' erecting warning signs everywhere, installing speed cameras, banning hobbies of which they disapprove, while in the meantime stripping away freedom after freedom and failing to confront the problems that the government were voted in to solve in the first place.

3 Health risks and safety hazard

They that can give up essential liberty to obtain a little temporary safety deserve neither liberty nor safety.

Benjamin Franklin, *Historical Review of Pennsylvania*, 1759

There was an unprecedented rise in the quality of living over the course of the twentieth century. Unfortunately, the massive improvements in healthcare that scientific advancement and dedicated research brought with them engendered the idea that we are constantly in great danger. Risks and diseases that would have been shrugged off by our ancestors were increasingly viewed as the gravest perils that face the human race. We, and especially our children, must be protected.

From the obesity 'epidemic' that is sweeping the Western World to the successive outbreaks of Salmonella, E-Coli, BSE or SARS; the sudden enormous dangers that our sexual activity presents us with, to the apparent impossibility of getting out of bed without contracting cancer in one of its many guises, modern life seems to have become almost impossibly dangerous. If one is to believe the government, the situation is destined to get even worse unless we abandon ourselves entirely to its recommendations. We are urged to give up ancient freedoms in order to increase, by even the tiniest percentage, our chances of staying alive for the maximum possible period in the least possible danger.

The huge increase in the Western world's perception of risk has coincided with the least risky period of our history. In the mid-nineteenth century, average life expectancy was 32 years for men and 30 for women, diseases such as smallpox were rife, and three in ten children died before reaching their first birthday. Yet commentators such as Carlyle wrote: 'To live under the reign of Victoria is to live for longer and better than any Englishman has had the good fortune.' The Victorians managed to face a worse world with a rosier world view than us. In the twenty-first century, despite the fact that the average life expectancy is 76 years for men and 81 for women, diseases such as smallpox have been eradicated, and the infant mortality rate is roughly five per thousand, we seem to be universally agreed that we live in one of the most dangerous periods of human history with absurd apocalyptic visions constantly being touted in the media.

In November 2001, Dr Peter Marsh of the Social Issues Research Centre in Oxford highlighted this irony when he wrote:

> Life is the safest it has ever been in the entire history of evolution. There is less disease, we are better fed and better protected, and our environment is safer. It's just a shame we

> feel compelled to invent fanciful fears to compensate for
> lack of real danger.

The 'fanciful fears' to which Dr. Marsh referred are on the increase. To keep up, the media run health scare stories on an almost daily basis, forcing people to question the very worth of their existence. Given the absurd amounts of danger that we apparently face, it may be futile to struggle against imminent death. The accuracy of the reporting, not to mention the accuracy of the 'scientific' studies on which the reports are usually based, is rarely called into question. In May 2003, however, a report into the media's exaggeration of the threat of the MMR vaccine was commissioned by the Economic and Social Research Council. The report concluded that the hysteria whipped up by the media was not even nearly justified by the overwhelming scientific consensus on the vaccine. The researchers, led by former *Independent* editor Ian Hargreaves, looked at 561 newspaper, radio and TV reports about MMR.

One of the authors of the study, Professor Justin Lewis, said:

> Our report shows that research questioning the safety of
> something...should be approached with caution, both by
> scientists and journalists. This is especially the case where
> any decline in confidence can have serious consequences
> for public health.

This understated criticism was not directed at any particular publication; the scaremongering had been universal. The papers, needless to say, paid no attention, and between May 2003 and May 2004 seemed to open up an industry-wide competition to see which publication could come up with the most ludicrous health scare.

On 13 May 2003, *The Guardian* opened the bidding with a report based on research at the Moredun Research Institute near Edinburgh which showed that animals such as 'horses, cows and pigs' posed an 'unknown risk' to humans. The scientists discovered that such animals 'could' be exposed to bacteria from the Chlamydia family which in turn 'could' be exposed to humans. The redundancy of the story was then admitted with the reiteration that the risk to humans remained 'unknown'.

Not to be outdone, *The Mirror* ran a story that day highlighting the enormous danger posed by 'rap' music. Listening to a song by Eminem whilst driving was discovered to be most likely to cause you to crash, according to 'car expert' Adam Verby. The basis of Mr. Verby's expertise was unclear. Nonetheless, a hundred drivers were tested and it was found that rap music was most likely to make you speed and drive dangerously. 'Pop' songs, however, were found to be good for concentration. Verby's ability to make a motor-neural distinction between the sound of Eminen and Madonna was remarkable, and remarkably unsound.

Two days later the *Daily Telegraph* (motto: 'Read a Bestseller Every Day') ran a story claiming that dishcloths were the latest terror to face the public. Its 'shock' survey revealed that nine out of ten dishcloths tested in restaurants were discovered to have been exposed to bacteria. Professor Eunice Taylor of the University of Salford pronounced: 'This demonstrates how far we have to go before the public can eat outside their home with the full assurance that what they are consuming will not make them ill.' Arguably, all it actually demonstrated was the reassuring truth that restaurants use dishcloths.

On 29 May, the *Daily Mail*, somewhat clutching at straws, asked: 'Is your bra bad for you?' It then told us why it could be: 'There is some evidence to associate wearing a bra with breast cancer, breathing problems, irritable bowl syndrome, back pain, circulation problems and skin problems.' Thankfully the *Mail,* not generally noted for its caution, fought shy of disclosing what the 'evidence' was, however.

As the year progressed, pointless exercises in scaremongering, misrepresentation and junk science continued. Of the proliferation of stories that came, some of the most preposterous dangers facing the public included:

BRUSHING TEETH: Peter Heasman at Newcastle University's School of Dental Sciences has found that brushing for longer than two minutes and with greater force does not improve oral hygiene and actually increases the risk of damage to teeth and gums. The professor of periodontology studied a dozen volunteers for four weeks. (*Times, Daily Telegraph, Guardian,* 19 June 2003)

BURGLARY: Elderly people who have been burgled are twice as likely to die early as non-victims. A Home Office study of 109 residents in sheltered housing in North Wales found that the health of those who had been victims of burglary deteriorated at an alarming rate. (*Daily Mail,* 26 June)

NIGHT SHIFTS: Almost half a million women who work night shifts could be at greater risk of breast cancer. Women who watch television late into the night, work night shifts or even sleep with a light on could be at risk because scientists believe that being exposed to too much light at night disrupts crucial hormones, raising the chances of breast tumours by as much as 60 per cent. (*Daily Mail,* 16 July)

TIES: Tightly knotted ties can increase the risk of glaucoma, an eye condition that is often hereditary and can cause blindness. Researchers at the New York Eye and Ear Infirmary tested 20 healthy men and 20 men with glaucoma and found that 60 per cent of the men with glaucoma and 70 per cent of the healthy men experienced an increase in internal eye blood pressure after wearing a tight tie for just three minutes. The study, published in the British Journal of Ophthalmology, also highlighted the problems of wearing a tie when going for an eye test where there was a risk it could lead to a false diagnosis of glaucoma. (*Independent,* 29 July)

BARBECUES: Barbecues should carry health warnings for releasing the same amount of toxic smoke as 220,000 cigarettes. Prof Desmond Hammerton, a retired biology professor from Callander, Scotland, said crowding round a barbecue throughout summer could have an effect 'over 10 or 20 years'. (*Sun,* 30 July)

MORTGAGES: Research from Sainsbury's Bank has said that the health of millions of mortgage holders is being affected because of fears over repayments. The bank claims that problems such as migraines and stress are affecting millions. (*Daily Express,* 7 August)

CELEBRITIES: A report in the *New Scientist* has warned of the dangers of 'Celebrity Worship Syndrome' that apparently affects one in three people. According to the authors of the study, following the lives of celebrities is a condition that is addictive and can escalate and become an unhealthy obsession. (*Telegraph, Mirror,* 14 August)

FAT DRIVERS: A study of 26,000 people involved in car accidents has found that those weighing between 15st 10lb and 18st 9lb were two and a half times more likely to die in a crash than people weighing less than 9st 6lb. (*Telegraph*, 16 August)

SUPERDADS: A leading psychiatrist has said that increasing numbers of fathers are seeking help for stress because of the pressures of being a 'new man'. These 'superdads' are overwhelmed by the weight of expectation of being the perfect employee, friend husband and father. The condition is described as the 'Atlas syndrome'. (*Daily Mail,* 25 August)

YOUNGEST IN CLASS: A study published in the British Medical Journal has shown that children who are among the youngest in their school year can be psychologically damaged by struggling to keep up. (*Guardian,* 29 August)

LIQUORICE: Eating too many liquorice allsorts, bootlaces and sherbet dabs could damage a man's sex drive, according to a new study. A team of Iranian scientists say the root – used in sweets, chewing gum, toothpaste and herbal gum – can lower testosterone levels. (*Daily Telegraph*)

MISERY: Feeling miserable? Don't, it's bad for your health! According to American scientists, people with a negative outlook are more likely to fall ill because their bodies have weaker immune systems which are less able to fight off infections. The findings, produced by the University of Wisconsin-Madison, are said to offer one of the best explanations yet for a phenomenon that doctors have observed for many years that people with an optimistic, happy-go-lucky approach to life tend to be healthier than those who are always miserable. (*Daily Mail, The Times,* 2 October)

BUDGET AIRLINES: Passengers flying budget airlines could be putting their lives in the hands of an exhausted pilot working a punishing flight schedule. Dr Simon Bennett of the University of Leicester said, 'While stress and fatigue are difficult to measure, and while the pilots' statements were informed by subjective self-assessments, it is clear that further research is required.' (*Independent,* 2 October)

TEXT MESSAGES: Dr Mark Collins of the Priory Hospital, London has said that more and more people are becoming addicted to text messaging. 'The main thing is about avoiding reality and living in an artificial reality.' (*Independent,* 6 October)

MODERN CULTURE: The nature of modern life is destroying people's memories. A survey has found that more than half of Britons cannot remember what they were doing last week. (*Daily Express ,* 7 October)

LONELINESS: A presentation at the American Heart Association's Scientific Sessions conference in Florida said that lonely old men are more at risk from a heart attack or stroke. (*Express,* 12 November)

MOBILES: Australian researchers have found that talking on a mobile phone while walking 'constitutes a serious health risk'. Chatting on the phone alters breathing patterns which usually protect the spine by cushioning footfall. The study, carried out on treadmill, found that the 'activity of the deepest abdominal muscle was reduced by 30-40 per cent during all speech tasks'. (*Daily Mail,* 18 November)

REFRIGERATORS: The arrival of domestic refrigerators could be responsible for a dramatic rise in the numbers suffering from a painful bowel disease over the last 50 years. According to Dr Jean-Pierre Hugot, who led the research in Paris, bacteria commonly found in beef, pork, chicken, cheese and lettuce may be to blame for Crohn's disease. Some of these bugs can survive and multiply in cold temperatures, contrary to the popular belief that fridges kill harmful bacteria. (*Daily Mail,* 11 December)

TELEVISION: Young children risk being 'damaged' by the excessively confrontational and sexual content of daytime television. Children's broadcasters, including Johnny Ball, Toni Arthur and Susan Stranks, say they are concerned that the depiction of warring adults and emotional trauma on programmes such as ITV's *Trisha* and Channel 4's *The Salon* could turn children into disturbed, self-obsessed adults with no understanding of happiness. (*Sunday Telegraph*, 1 February 2004)

MOBILE PHONE MASTS: Plans by BT to erect hundreds of thousands of mini mobile phone masts on street lights, road signs and buildings has enraged opponents who say radiation can cause cancer, brain damage, Alzheimer's disease, loss of memory and sleep disorder. Although there are no scientific studies linking mast radiation to ill health, the consumer group Mast Sanity said, 'These masts could be extremely dangerous, as we won't know they are there.' (*Daily Mail,* 6 February 2004)

ORAL SEX: Oral sex can lead to oral tumours. Researchers, working for the International Agency for Research on Cancer in Lyon, France, compared 1670 patients who had oral cancer with 1732 healthy volunteers. The risk, however, is miniscule. Only around 1 in 10,000 people develop oral tumours each year, and most cases are probably caused by two other popular recreational pursuits: smoking and drinking. The researchers are not recommending any changes in behaviour. (*New Scientist*, 25 February 2004)

Often such stories are rendered harmless by their own mindless stupidity. The idea that being the youngest in class constitutes a 'health risk' is meaningless because it is an unavoidable predicament for one child in every classroom in the country. As a result, no one who read the article gave it a moment's serious thought. Quite probably, no one read the article at all. Sometimes, however, stories were used to scaremonger in the most irresponsible way, exaggerating statistics and extrapolating shocking headlines from entirely innocuous reports. Witness the *Daily Mail* story about mobile telephone masts. The report accepted that there was no scientific evidence that the masts were dangerous but a spokesman for the cleverly named group, Mast Sanity, expressed outrage nevertheless. In truth, most health scare 'stories' are lent weight by attention-seeking psychiatrists, health care 'experts' or safety 'professionals' seeking their few minutes in the limelight. Alternatively, cash-starved university research departments conduct half-baked 'research' to attract the attention of bored newspaper editors.

There is a problem that goes deeper than poor journalism, though. The sheer number of unfounded 'scares' reported by the media lends the issue an iniquitous and undeserved weight. Our innate reason dismisses ridiculous 'warnings' individually, but their persistent mass appearance has the same effect as a lurking fog. You can't quite see it, and if you cast about you it seems to evaporate, but you are left with the creeping conviction that it's *out there*. Naturally enough, perspective is lost between genuine health concerns and those that are nothing more than the excited fantasies of tabloid-appointed 'experts'. That lost perspective is one that the Nanny State is then able to exploit.

The relationship between the Nanny State and the media is a curious one. On the one hand, the media, particularly the right wing media, condemn too much government intervention, with *The Sun* and *The Mail* commenting that some new legislation is an example of the 'Nanny State gone mad!' on an almost daily basis. On the other hand, however, the same newspapers habitually blow any reported health scare wildly out of proportion, gladly confuse 'junk' scientific reports with reports that may have value, and gleefully protest that the government must do something.

This actually forces the state into a difficult position, as it is damned whatever it does; if it ignores the scare stories it will be accused of being irresponsible, but if it acts on them it will be accused of nannying. By the same papers, too. Generally, however, the government heeds the messages of the various ridiculous stories, and gives in to its love of bossing people around.

Often the subsequent legislation goes beyond parody. Wiltshire County Council, for example, interpreted the 'news' that harmful bacteria 'can' develop in fresh food which, in turn, 'might' cause humans slight stomach upsets as an imperative to ban children from bringing homemade cakes to school. Thus are tiny, but nonetheless vital, liberties gently eroded. The government restrictions extended to fresh meat, fish and anything containing cream, eggs or mayonnaise. Such dangerous child-killing substances were to be replaced by safer foodstuffs such as shop-bought cakes, jam and pre-packed processed food, preferably purchased from top donor Sainsbury's.

In obedience with the new legislation, Lisa Tudor, headmistress of Crudwell Church of England Primary School in Wiltshire declared through clenched teeth:

> ...we will be unable to receive homemade food products for distribution. We cannot hold cake stalls selling homemade cakes. If it is a child's birthday we can only accept shop-bought products.

The measures were virtually guaranteed to reduce pupils' initiative and enthusiasm, and further test the worryingly thin patience of bewildered parents, one of whom showed sufficient fortitude to joke that '...this is really taking the biscuit'. Wiltshire County Council were unrepentant, however, and pledged that they would continue to put the prevention of ridiculously unlikely health hazards above decent education. A spokesman pointed out: '...shops and retailers have very strict rules. You wouldn't buy a cream cake that had been sitting in the sun all day from a supermarket, so we shouldn't be selling them at school fêtes.' The fact that Crudwell School was neither a shop nor a retailer was deemed irrelevant. The council appeared to miss the entire point of a primary school fête, namely to encourage children and their parents to create something together which could then be sold in an atmosphere of goodwill for the benefit of the community.

In Norwich, a council with a similar attitude towards child safety had an avenue of twenty horse chestnut trees felled. In the conker season, children might have been tempted to throw sticks at the trees to bring down the conkers. In the process, they were incurring the terrifying risk of the sticks falling down from the trees and landing on someone's head. The ruling was passed, as much of such health and safety legislation is, not because pedestrians had complained about the number of unconscious children that littered the roadside, but because some self-important member of the council had 'identified a potential problem'. Arguably, absurdly over-protected children incapable of dealing with eventualities as unthreatening as falling twigs are a greater 'potential problem'.

Such patronising nonsense is not just confined to children, either. Figures from the Department of Trade and Industry released in 2002 showed that seventy people were killed and two-hundred-and-fifty thousand injured in the UK as they tackled DIY Projects. The DTI decided that, because this figure was marginally up on the year before, and because programmes such as 'Changing Rooms' had recently become popular, the two facts were related. Furthermore, the television programmes must be at fault. The Consumer Affairs Minister, Kim Howells said, 'It looks easy on TV and people are always over-reaching themselves.' Two million 'safety' leaflets issued by the DTI were then given away at DIY stores across the country at considerable expense. Official DTI figures for how many extra beds could have been created in NHS hospitals for the same sum are not yet available.

The charming Suffolk seaside town of Felixstowe suffered particularly from the onslaught of the health and safety craze. 'The Nanny State gone absolutely berserk,' was how Doreen Savage, the mayor of the town, described the mosaic of safety signs which were rapidly erected along the length of the town's previously attractive sea wall. The signs were put up by the Environment Agency as part of their campaign 'Operation Public Safety', to warn the public that falling off the wall might be dangerous. 'No one', said Mrs Savage has ever fallen off our sea wall. 'Putting up twenty signs where one would do is just a joke.'

The Environment Agency was unrepentant, however, and pledged that, following a nationwide survey of fifty thousand agency assets, it would be erecting thousands of new signs across the country. The signs are so ugly that the campaign may prove even more effective than the EA intended, as scenic areas are rendered so garishly ugly that tourists will keep well clear of them in future.

While it is easy to lampoon the government and the excitable little enforcers of the Nanny State, there are, of course, genuine dangers from which it is the responsible society's duty to protect its members. However, like the little boy crying wolf, the Nanny State's suggestion that every aspect of our daily lives is potentially lethal leads people into a false sense of security when confronting genuine threats to their health and safety. This is not helped by the fact that, on the rare occasions when the government's intervention to counter a safety threat is actually welcome, it vastly exaggerates the dangers posed, relying on the resulting hysteria to do its work for it.

This method was at the fore of the 'epidemic' of obesity announced at the beginning of 2004. Instead of accepting that rising obesity levels are entirely the fault of lazy slobs eating rubbish while sitting in front of the television all day instead of doing any exercise, the government were desperate to pin the blame on the 'concerted efforts of the junk food industry'. Finding big corporations to blame had the added bonus of giving capitalism and globalisation a public kicking while providing the premise for the introduction of new 'fat' taxes. Forcing up the price of junk food doesn't stop people eating it, however, it just makes them spend more money on it, so they get both fatter and poorer. As always, the easiest social group to leap to the defence of was children, and 'childhood obesity' quickly became the new national obsession, with acres of newspaper coverage devoted to what was universally described as an 'epidemic'.

The newspapers' old habit of exaggerating statistics and misrepresenting scientific studies brought ever more startling predictions to the breakfast tables of the nation – where the traditional bacon and eggs was quickly replaced with yoghurt and muesli. On 12 February, *The Independent* ran a front page story announcing that 'doctors' had warned of a 'terrifying rise in obesity'. It claimed: 'Children as young as six are developing breathing problems, irreversible biological changes, and type two diabetes, a disease previously only seen in overweight, middle-aged adults.' The paper cited a report, published by the Royal College of Physicians, the Royal College of Paediatrics and Child Health and the Faculty of Public Health, comparing it to a landmark study in 1962 by the Royal College of Physicians which first outlined the health risks associated with smoking.

Predictably enough, obesity was conclusively linked to cancer within a month, the *Daily Telegraph* reported on 6 April:

> Obesity could overtake smoking as the most common preventable cause of cancer within ten years…a third of all cancers will be linked to excess fat by the middle of the next decade unless the obesity epidemic can be halted. Studies have shown that being overweight increases the risk of cancer of the breast, womb, kidney, bowel and oesophagus.

Newspapers often do not bother to stand up theses scare stories to anyone more specific than 'scientists' or 'doctors'. This can lead to wildly contradictory stories sharing column space, as demonstrated by the reports towards the end of 2002 that Britain was suffering from undernourishment and malnutrition. To be suffering from obesity and starvation epidemics simultaneously would not just be a crisis, it would be a miracle. *The Mirror* nevertheless reported on the twelfth of November that 'two million Britons are so underfed that they could be classed as malnourished' and that 'forty per cent of those admitted to hospital are underweight and sixty per cent of those already in hospital are malnourished.'

The intervening eighteen months gave the millions of

malnourished a chance to catch up and swing the scales in the other direction. The sinister-sounding 'junk food industry' would have to have made very concerted efforts indeed to bring about such a rapid reversal alone. In May 2004, figures were released showing that one in ten six-year-olds and one in five fifteen-year-olds were obese. The damage done to their infant metabolism as they veered between emaciation and corpulence must have been incalculable. Professor Mike Kelly, the Director of the Health Development Agency, told the *Telegraph* that it was a result of the 'Obesogenic' environment in which the children were brought up, exposed to fast food and the 'couch potato culture'. Where this left the 'undernourishment' culture of less than two years earlier was anybody's guess.

It was inevitable that the fast food industry would get the blame, and much noise was made about the introduction of new 'fat' taxes to punish the purveyors of fattening foods. McDonald's in particular began a swift campaign to change their image. 'We're lovin' it' became the chain's new slogan, and all its stores were quickly painted a slimming cream instead of the old cartoonish red and yellow. A line of 'McSalads' was introduced as well, although it remained largely unpublicised that their dressing contained more fat than a Big Mac. They would need more than an extremely sugary salad to fool the press, however, who had already identified deep fried chips and greasy burgers as the enemy.

The *Daily Mail* decided that Ronald McDonald was responsible for even more than mere obesity. 'Eating junk food harms the memory and may even lead to brain damage,' the paper announced, basing its claims on a study carried out by the University of

California's Brain Injury Research Centre and published in the journal *Neuroscience*. People who enjoy burgers could be 'unwittingly harming their minds', the paper gleefully reported. The irony of such a piece appearing in the most 'mind-harming' tabloid in Britain was not lost on many.

The Express trumped even the *Mail*, extending the obesity epidemic to pets. 'A growing number of household pets, including cats, dogs, rabbits and budgies, are getting dangerously fat because their owners are feeding them junk food. According to the Blue Cross charity, the number of overweight animals has doubled in the last ten years. Fat pets are more likely to die young or suffer from illnesses including breathlessness, diabetes, arthritis and heatstroke.'

As if the sound of fat budgies wobbling breathless from their perches because of their owners' insistence on feeding them pizzas rather than seeds wasn't enough, the media's own squawking had reached fever pitch. Nanny was standing back and paying no attention as the children gorged themselves to death, seemed to be the implication. So, ever eager to please, the government commissioned a report.

The House of Commons Health Select Committee's report into obesity, published on 27 May, brought home the full horror of the problem by highlighting the case of a three-year-old Bengali girl who had died in a London hospital of heart failure 'where extreme obesity was a contributory factor'. The unfortunate toddler was then disgustingly, and misleadingly, described as 'choking on her own fat.' The Select Committee, with considerable artistic licence, extrapolated from this horrific incident the following bleak view of the future in overweight Britain:

> The sight of amputees will become much more
> familiar. There will be many more blind people. There
> will be huge demand for kidney dialysis… Indeed, this
> will be the first generation where children die before
> their parents as a consequence of childhood obesity.'

The reaction to the report was immediate, with every newspaper's headline screaming a preposterous message of doom. Predictably, the *Daily Mail* led the field in sanctimoniousness, suggesting that the parents of the three-year-old girl should be 'charged with nothing less than child abuse'. The newspaper's readers offered equally considered opinions on its online discussion board. The parents were 'too thick' to have children, 'hated' their children, or actively 'wished them dead' according to various *Mail* journalists posing as members of the public.

Once the hysteria died down and people went back to their usual diet of deep-fried breakfasts and over-sugared tea, the truth emerged, very quietly. The girl had died from an extremely rare genetic condition and her obesity and heart failure had nothing to do with either her parents' neglect or the corrupt and gluttonous society in which she had lived. Her condition stemmed from birth and was terminal. Her appearance in the Select Committee's report on obesity was nothing less than a gross abuse of public trust. Contemptibly, her supposed relevance was dependent on a complete misrepresentation of the facts. However, when taken up on the issue, David Hinchcliffe, who chaired the health committee, claimed that the inclusion of the girl's story in the report on obesity did not say or imply that the girl died from overeating. The chairman of the National Obesity Forum went on to say that the misrepresentation must not be used to 'distract attention from the root point'. The fact that the 'epidemic' of obesity could only be demonstrated by misrepresenting the truth had grave implications for the Select Committee. They considered themselves justified in scapegoating a tragic infant and exposing her family to severe public opprobrium to draw attention to the 'root point'. They were determined to use any means necessary to raise public awareness of the problem they were being paid to assess. Any logical analysis of such behaviour leads inexorably to the real 'root point'. There is no obesity epidemic, other than in the terribly overstaffed and overstuffed corridors of Whitehall.

Such dishonesty demonstrates the danger of a government which uses the level of media outrage as a sounding board for whether or not it can get away with intrusive legislation. If it senses that the public's outrage is great enough for the public to welcome legislation, it acts – even if it has to rely on bogus statistics to justify the new legislation to those of a less hysterical disposition than the average *Mail* reader.

Another example is the move to outlaw smoking. Nobody would ever suggest that smoking is anything other than extremely bad for you. Anybody with any intuition who has ever tried inhaling a cigarette can feel exactly why it is so dangerous. The decision to smoke, therefore, is one taken by the smoker, in the full knowledge that what he is doing could harm him. The same argument could be made for those who enjoy parachuting out of aeroplanes or deep-sea diving. They know the risks, but wish to enjoy a life which embraces that risk. Such an attitude to life, however, is one that the Nanny State particularly despises, and always aims to eradicate.

The success of the ban on smoking in public places in Ireland has led to calls for such a ban to come into effect here. The main argument against smoking in public is that passive smoking is almost as dangerous a killer as smoking itself. A campaign in California promoting this depicts a man holding a cigarette at a café leaning towards a woman and asking politely, 'Mind if I smoke?' The woman's absurd response is 'Care if I die?'

The extent of the danger of passive smoking has never been agreed upon, and the idea that banning smoking would prevent people from inhaling carcinogenic substances is ridiculous. Walking along any high street, whether one smokes or not, means exposing the lungs to all sorts of horrible emissions. The *Daily Express* on 12 November 2003 claimed that 'after completing tests in the Marylebone Road, a report has found that walking in big cities is the equivalent of smoking a cigarette every two and a half minutes. Experts say that pollution kills around 40,000 Britons every year.' Whether or not this report is reliable, it at least demonstrates that passive smoking is not the only danger that non-smokers are exposed to and that the outcry against smokers when a non-smoker occasionally contracts lung cancer may not be entirely balanced.

There is something about people who choose to smoke, even though they know it to be bad for them, that the Nanny State cannot understand or tolerate, and the anti-smoking lobby will only be happy when the habit is extinguished completely. This is demonstrated by the fact that the perfectly reasonable proposals that restaurants and bars are obliged to have a designated 'no-smoking' zone have been rejected by the lobby. Not content with merely taxing smokers more than in any other country on Earth, the health crusaders then passed a law stating that all packets of cigarettes and tobacco must be covered in disgusting warning signs reminding smokers of such grim facts as that 'Smoking Kills!', 'Smoking Reduces Sperm Count' and other such extraneous bits of information. The lobby now wish to go further, and instead of just having printed warnings on cigarettes, they want to have pictures of diseased mouths and lungs on the packets.

Furthermore, smokers are submitted to perhaps the most intensive health propaganda campaign that the media has ever waged. Newspaper reports in 2004 alone have linked smoking to Alzheimer's disease, susceptibility to frostbite, infertility, senile dementia, miscarriage and cervical cancer, early menopause, breast cancer, the low-fertility of the smoker's offspring, multiple sclerosis and other auto-immune diseases, giving birth to 'jittery, excitable and stiff' babies, and depression.

One of the major problems with all this, aside from the sheer waste of money, time and people's patience the whole thing causes, is the fact that there is no sensible end to it. Once some bright spark has decided that something is harmful, and procures funding for researching their claim, which is then inevitably proved, resulting in a recommendation for immediate legislation, they have nothing more to do. So they invent another health risk, procure the funding, conduct the research and recommend more legislation.

In order for these people to remain employed, they have to make sure that this cycle is repeated indefinitely. As a result, the sensible safety measures which are initially introduced by legislation escalate out of all reason as the enforcers of health and safety make ever more desperate bids to cling onto their jobs.

A good example of this is with driving. Twenty years ago, on 31 January 1983, the regulation that all front seat drivers must wear seatbelts was introduced and in 1992 the law was extended to those sitting in the rear seats. Although there was minor complaint about the government's bossiness at the time, the measures could not really be viewed as a restriction of people's freedom, and it is realistically estimated that the measure has saved over fifty thousand lives and over half-a-million serious injuries since its introduction. Clearly, the introduction of seatbelts was a success, and as such, should not be considered the action of a Nanny State. It made sense and has probably saved thousands of lives.

Then, however, speeding came under the microscope, and increasingly intrusive measures have been introduced to stop people from breaking the speed limits, including the speed cameras that now punctuate almost every street. Again, there is an undoubted benefit in people driving at a sensible speed. However, there is clear evidence that speed cameras are over-zealously deployed by the police to meet government-specified efficiency 'targets'. Speed cameras are also extremely lucrative. They were initially justified as a method of controlling accident 'black spots', as if their life-saving purpose was their only function. Their subsequent placement has often seemed extremely eccentric, however. For instance, two cameras on the A46 approach to Bath were deliberately concealed behind a bridge at the bottom of a very steep hill at exactly the point where the speed limit changes from 60 to 50 mph. Not only was the speed limit change signalled at the same point where the cameras were hidden, but the area itself was a pedestrian-free dual carriageway with no 'black spot' credentials. Given that it was almost impossible not to be snapped by the cameras at the foot of the hill without dangerously applying the brake, motorists were left wondering who these 'safety devices' were really there for.

At sixty quid a pop, they certainly benefited North East Somerset County Council handsomely, but in the absence of any accidents either before or after (although possibly not during) their instalment, they were of no obvious service to the community. The only reassuring aspect was that they were triggered so frequently that camera film was used up faster than the council could replace it, creating a momentarily blinding safety hazard for drivers without even being able to record their virtually unavoidable crime.

The Sun finally ran an article asking, 'Are these the most unfair speed cameras in Britain?' which prompted their eventual removal. In the absence of any council justification or apology, however, their legacy was simply further erosion of respect for government authority. And an enormous swelling of the local council's coffers.

The next measure to be introduced, as a means of coercing those who still insist on speeding, is the sleeping policemen, and other traffic calming measures that are being set up in towns all over the country. Of course speeding in residential areas is dangerous and anti-social, but the extraordinary amount of humps, bumps, chicanes, extended pavements and painted signs on streets is quite obviously daft as well as bewildering and a safety hazard itself. The London

Ambulance Service estimates that about five hundred lives are lost a year due to traffic calming measures slowing down ambulances. Fire engine drivers experience a similar thwarting which sometimes prevents them doing their work at all. As the life-saving vehicles slow from a race to a crawl in residential areas, the distant cries of burning people slowly fade as the flames do their work. The drivers are specifically trained to drive at high speeds in residential areas, and are less likely than anyone to run down an innocent child. The dreadful possibility must be legislated for, however, over and above the rather more dreadful actuality of people being burned to death. A further useful deployment of government money might be to employ stuntmen to show ambulance drivers and firemen how to whiz over obstacles Dukes of Hazard-style, reducing the problem they pose to those trying to save lives.

Whether or not these measures do, on balance, save more lives than they endanger, is open to debate. However, it is obvious that the campaigning by the road safety fanatics has begun to lose its grasp on reality. Their next obsession was the danger of mobile telephones to drivers, and legislation was swiftly introduced to ban their use in cars in December 2003, with a maximum penalty of £2500. Hands-free phones are, so far, exempt from this legislation. It was pointed out by the Department for Transport that, under Regulation 104 of the Road Vehicles (Construction and Use) Regulations of 1986, the police would still be able to prosecute if a driver was to have an accident while speaking on a hands-free device, so there is, inevitably, a movement gaining momentum for their prohibition as well. This constant chipping away at the freedom of the motorist can only head towards absurdity. The argument for banning hand-held mobiles is that the driver is not concentrating fully on the road and has one hand off the wheel. The argument for banning hands-free kits is that talking on a phone means that the driver is not concentrating fully on the road. In fact, bizarrely, a report by the UK Transport Research Laboratory (TRL) released on 22 March 2002 managed to prove that talking on a phone, even on a hands-free kit, is more dangerous than driving when drunk. While the 'scientific' study into this proved it 'conclusively', it is obvious, even to someone who is very drunk, that it is not true. Even if talking on a mobile phone is highly dangerous, it cannot be more so than having to silence warring children on the back seat, or looking at a map for directions – neither of which have been specifically targeted for legislation. The logic, if pursued, must ultimately entail the banning of all passengers in cars, because presumably they offer a distraction for drivers in the same way that mobile phones do. Once passengers are banned in cars, the fanatics would have to start worrying about something else, perhaps the dangers of listening to music in cars. Furthermore, the environmentalists would be even more upset by the resultant massive increase in cars.

The irony of all this is that it can only actually make driving *more* dangerous, as all this legislation against driving effectively reduces the responsibility that a driver has to take for his own actions. It implies that the critical faculties essential to driving are mere reflexes, as though drivers were laboratory rats, or autonomous robots. Removing all possible risk from driving may sound sensible, but it is ultimately counter-productive, as managing risk is what driving is all about. The proposal that cars are all fitted with GPS tracking devices which would enable speed limits to be imposed on drivers automatically, for example, might sound clever, but it would potentially invite greater danger, as in the instances were a driver can only avoid an accident by accelerating to escape it.

This inane trend towards blanket legislation banning everything that could possibly be viewed as a potential risk to health and safety is clearly a waste of time, but it is also a huge waste of money, and it is perhaps in examining this that one can identify the more sinister motivations behind the Nanny State.

Every Wednesday, the Guardian carries a heavy supplement entitled Society. In one issue, selected at random, the following positions were advertised: Older People Services Director, Youth Service Manager, Head of Healthy Living and Sport, Supporting People Project Officer, Consents Manager, Rural Renaissance Manager, Five-a-Day Co-ordinator, Positive Action Worker, Team Leader (Sustainability), Lesbian, Gay and Bisexual Youth Worker, Antisocial Behaviour Co-ordinator, Neighbourhood Facilitation Advisor, Smoking Cessation officer, Senior Parent Advisor, and Senior Play Development Officer. The list goes on...and on...and on, for a hundred and seventeen pages.

It is no surprise that Nanny's in-house newspaper is called *The Guardian*. An independent study reported in the *Daily Mail* in January 2004 revealed that than two thirds of the government's advertising budget for public sector jobs is spent on the pages of its 'Society' supplement. Part of the reason for all of this is that 'New' Labour identified some time ago that the way to increase employment and, indeed, head the country towards full employment, is through inventing unnecessary posts such as these and then filling them with those who will inevitably remain loyal to the government that fosters the Nanny State. This idea was one basically copied from the Soviet Union whose enormous bureaucracy created an absurdly top-heavy, expensive and cumbersome state whose only consolation was to boast of its full employment figures.

The similar thinking between the Soviet Union and the idealists behind the Nanny State are demonstrated in the conclusions of a conference on 'Economic Policies for Full Employment and Defence of the Welfare State', held at Congress House on December 1994. John Edmonds, the general secretary of the GMB (the general union), praised the Full Employment Forum for its victory in the battle of ideas:

> We have transformed the labour movement's political agenda. At the 1992 general election, full employment wasn't an issue, but John Smith's speech to the 1993 TUC Conference, at which he signalled the Labour leadership's commitment to full employment, was a turning point...
>
> It is not difficult for socialists to identify obvious areas of unmet social need. The work to do is everywhere: in the environment, health and safety, counselling, transport regulation and caring for the socially excluded and the elderly. But the market won't create jobs. Both initial economic stimulus by government and a commitment on its part to carry policies through would be necessary; so it must occasionally borrow money to stimulate the economy.

How such an irresponsible redistribution of wealth could ever be seen to 'stimulate the economy' is a mystery. Health and safety officials, transport regulators, and those 'carers' of the 'socially excluded and the elderly', even where their work is actually of value, do not help generate money other than in providing an excuse to introduce new taxes, therefore they cannot stimulate the economy, they can only drain it.

The Health and Safety Executive, specifically, illustrates how far this process has gone. It now requires over four thousand employees and £200 million a year to run the department that enforced the recent 'triumphs' such as the banning of mobiles in cars, the felling of conker trees and the requirement that circus performers must wear hard hats if working above the height of a normal stepladder.

The HSE, and its supervisory quango, the Health and Safety Commission, claim that they are merely administering the law as laid down by Parliament. But its role has gradually drifted from the impartiality it exercised when run by scientists and civil servants to a more politicised one. An obvious example of this was the attempt by the HSE to prosecute the current and previous Commissioners of the Metropolitan Police, Sir John Stevens and Lord Condon, for the death of Hayes policeman PC Kulwant Sidhu, aged 24, in October 1999.

PC Sidhu died accidentally after falling through a roof while chasing criminals. The HSE spent over three million pounds of public funds on the case for prosecution, arguing that Condon and Stevens, through allowing policeman to chase criminals across roofs, had failed to ensure the young officer's safety. Luckily, the prosecution failed. Had it succeeded, however, Stevens said that there would have been 'irreparable damage' to policing in Britain. He noted:

> This result is a victory for good sense and will allow us to
> continue to deliver an effective policing service to the
> public... I would wish to make it absolutely clear that I am
> a staunch supporter of sensible, balanced health and safety
> measures for police officers. During my time as a chief
> officer I have always sought to work with Health and Safety
> experts to ensure the highest possible safety standards for
> staff. Indeed, safety is at the core of the police service at
> every level.

As the commissioner argued, health and safety is obviously
important to policing, as it is to all areas of life. However, when such
a noble sentiment is hijacked by phoney political idealists who have
identified a new means to spend public money, irritate people and
pursue a selfish agenda which has no benefit to health, safety or the
economy, questions should surely be being asked about the real
intentions and advantages of our burgeoning Nanny State.

4 **Monsters under the bed**

The whole aim of practical politics is to keep the populace
alarmed (and hence clamorous to be led to safety) by menacing
it with an endless series of hobgoblins, all of them imaginary

H. L. Mencken

Whaile it is an old device for the parents or nannies of unruly children to scare them into behaving themselves with tales of bogeymen who will haunt them if they don't do as they are told, the idea that a government could use the same tactic on an adult population seems absurd. Recently, however, it appears to have become accepted ministerial practice, as the government again looks to the nursery for inspiration for its policies.

As with the recent spate of scare stories about risks to our health and safety, the media are only too delighted to give credibility to the government's latest obsession, so much so that the readers of most newspapers would be forgiven for never daring to leave their houses, because they must be so terrified of the legions of paedophiles, rapists, crazed gunmen, and Islamic terrorists roaming our streets. Having frightened the people sufficiently for them to abandon rational thought and agree to the due processes of democracy and justice being repealed to tackle the latest supposed 'emergency', the government is then in a position to do what it loves to do best: legislate. New laws are passed and teams of meddling bureaucrats are employed at the public's expense to enforce them. Jobs are thus 'created' and remain in place even after the imagined threat is long forgotten.

It is for this reason that the government makes such a big issue out of the odd 'atrocity' that tragically, but inevitably, occurs. No government can change the fact that monstrous crimes are, occasionally, committed by unstable or evil people. The fact that human beings can, in extreme cases, sink to the vilest depths of depravity is an unchangeable one. However, it is this intangible aspect of human nature that also allows for extreme genius or selfless bravery and is one that has to be accepted as a necessary part of a free existence. Reactionary and rushed legislation in the wake of atrocities tends to target scapegoats rather than causes, and more often than not is brought in expediently to tackle problems that have nothing to do with what prompted their introduction.

One constant remains in the introduction of such legislation, however – the persistent infringement of civil liberties.

In response to criticism of some of the more extreme measures proposed in the aftermath of 9/11, the Home Secretary, David Blunkett, summed up the government's position starkly, 'We can live in a world with airy-fairy civil liberties and believe the best in everybody and they destroy us. But that's not the world we live in.'

Even in the face of a significant terrorist threat, the idea that the notion of civil liberties is an 'airy–fairy' one is a pointer to the true illiberality of our Nanny's outlook on the world.

Within any state, there is of course a balance to be met between liberty and security, and it is a balance that the citizen must be expected to accept. This has been argued since the time of Hobbes, and it is within this context that Blair's favourite soundbite that 'there cannot be rights without responsibilities' actually has some resonance. However, criminal or terrorist outrages, which by their very nature are extremely rare, must be dealt with within the terms of such a balance and must never be used as an excuse to tilt that balance in the direction of security over freedom. While they must be examined and their cause identified, irresponsible attributions of blame and witchhunts for scapegoats is not the way of good governance.

Blunkett's lofty dismissal of civil liberties in the aftermath of the World Trade Centre attacks could perhaps be excused in the face of imminent apocalypse. As a considered response to the actual chain of events, however, they were wilfully extreme, and exposed a casual disregard for both the idea of freedom and the true nature of the complicated problems facing the West in the aftermath of the attacks.

Furthermore, using such outrages as an excuse to tighten the state's grip on the private lives of the individual implies that doing so will make a difference, and guarantee our future security. Of course, it can't and, as with much of the Nanny State's interference, if a new policy or 'emergency measure' cannot prove its own worth by its effectiveness, it is valueless, and, therefore, a waste of legislative process, money and time. Wasting time on irrelevancies is often Nanny's preferred occupation, though, particularly when confronted with shocking realities like child murder.

Child's Play 3 : Chucky's Revenge was not generally considered a great film. The average viewer would in fact be forgiven for not remembering anything about it at all. It was therefore surprising to see it become, albeit briefly, the most notorious example of depraved popular culture in Britain in the wake of the conviction of two children, Robert Thomson and Jon Venables, for the murder of two-year-old James Bulger in 1993.

The *Daily Mail* responsibly branded the killers 'freaks of nature', whilst *The Mirror* showed its customary restraint by calling them 'evil, pure evil'. The media united in pointing the finger at a low-budget, low-grade horror film about a malevolent doll, unanimously declaring that the film's terrible depravity had directly inspired the boys to kill someone themselves. The evidence for such a theory was almost non-existent. In his summing up, Mr. Justice Morland had merely mentioned that the killers '...exposure to violent video films may in part be an explanation'. But *The Sun* quickly discovered that one of the killers' fathers had once rented *Child's Play 3*. There was no evidence whatsoever that either Thomson or Venables had watched it, Thomson's favourite film being *The Goonies*, but tabloid headlines cried 'Ban Sick Chucky Film Now!' The *Sun* itself pleaded 'For the sake of all our kids, burn this video nasty!'

Merseyside Police, for what it was worth, issued their own press release stating: '...we dismiss any link – if you are going to link this murder to a film, you might as well link it to *The Railway Children*.' But in times of media derangement a scapegoat must be found, and the Home Secretary, Michael Howard, attempted to make a practical contribution to the hysteria by fining video shop owners who supplied '15' and '18' certificate videos to children below the ages of fifteen and eighteen. The gesture was largely hollow because the majority of underage viewers of violent films do not rent them personally, but then the film itself was clearly not the root cause of the murder in any event.

Ironically, the single fact of the case that so appalled the nation – that Jamie Bulger had been a child, incapable of properly understanding what was happening to him – did not generate any sympathy for the accused, of whom the same was true. Thomson and Venables were tried in an adult courtroom, albeit one in which the dock had to be raised by three inches to allow them to see over the rail. Social workers, though, did hold their hands.

The defence argued that the publicity surrounding the case had been so prejudicial that the boys couldn't possibly receive a fair trial. Assembled were two hundred and forty seven press cuttings, including comparisons of the boys (who were aged ten at the time of the killing) with Saddam Hussein, and a pixelated photo from *The Sun* of them sucking lollipops on the courtroom steps, 'without a care in the world'.

The trial, however, went ahead as if they were adults. The boys were present throughout, but they may as well not have been – their lawyers weren't specialist child lawyers, and never consulted their clients. There was an obvious inconsistency that the two boys were perceived to lack the maturity to instruct their lawyers but were considered mature enough to commit murder with a full understanding of its implications.

Outside the courtroom, the moral hysteria continued. On the 25th November, *The Guardian* recorded that 'within minutes of the jury reaching guilty verdicts at Preston crown court, a Commons motion was tabled calling for a Home Office investigation into the role that TV and video violence played in creating the psychological impulses for this murder.' David Alton MP, never slow to comment on 'moral' issues, was quoted in *The Sun* as saying, 'our homes have been penetrated by garbage. If you dress murder and rape as entertainment, how can a child know right from wrong?'

In retrospect, the most significant 'contributor' to the debate was the then junior Shadow Transport Secretary, Tony Blair. He described the murder as an '...ugly manifestation of a society that is becoming unworthy of the name', adding that the availability of films like *Child's Play 3 : Chucky's Revenge* was '...a hammer-blow against the sleeping conscience of the country'. He proposed that its supply should be prohibited not just to children, but to everybody. In one of the first recorded instances of his characteristic formulation, he said that people '...can't have rights without responsibilities'. Nobody realised that what he actually believed was that people can't have rights.

Despite all of the moral outrage and frenzied tabloid doom-mongering *Child's Play 3 : Chucky's Revenge* is still available.

Miraculously, the death toll has not increased as a result.

The furore over the 'video nasties' was almost identical to the outrage at the 'penny dreadfuls' that were popular with Victorian youngsters. Of these, Thomas Wright, a writer on working-class life, said in 1881, 'It often happens, we are aware, that some juvenile till-robber is found to be a reader of penny dreadfuls. Nevertheless, we cannot agree with the conclusion usually taken in these cases that the reading and robbery stand in the relation of cause and effect.'

Such common sense has continued to be rejected ever since, and the latest plague to poison our children's minds was identified in July 2004, when seventeen-year-old Warren Leblanc pleaded guilty to the murder of fourteen-year-old Stefan Pakeerah. The mother of the victim, Giselle Pakeerah, pointed to the killer's 'obsession' with the videogame *Manhunt* as the cause of her son's death.

The media reaction that followed was predictably restrained. 'Obsessed teen guilty of brutal copycat murder' screamed *The Mirror*. The victim's uncle was reported as comparing *Manhunt* to 'child pornography' and the *Daily Mail* ran a two-page spread given over to 'Murder by Playstation: horror images on computer drove teenager to kill his friend'. The following day's *Mail* did not report the exact number of murders that had been inspired by the game's violent images, but implied that a cyberspace serial killer was on the loose.

The high-street chain Dixon's managed to do its duty as both a responsible retailer and a publicity-hungry business by banning *Manhunt* from its shelves immediately. It is not known whether or not Leblanc bought the game from a branch of Dixon's, but it would have been prudent for him to do so, as prior to the sudden discovery of the danger posed by the game, the store had been encouraging children to buy it by selling it for twenty pounds less than its recommended retail price.

The *Sun* expressed its righteous outrage at the 'Sicko Games Scandal' on 30 July, devoting a full-page review to 'the most bloodthirsty games on the market'. Reporter Johnathan Weinberg spent a day playing nine such games, including *Manhunt*, of which he said, 'The better you get at playing the game, the more bloody and nasty it gets.'

While he was wearing down his thumbs on the control pad of his Playstation, his colleague Grant Rollings instead encouraged two 'underage investigators' of sixteen and fourteen to buy these murder-inducing games in London stores. Shockingly, 'every one sold a gory game to at least one of the boys – even though some stores, with Dixons leading the way, had banned *Manhunt* from their shelves'.

The paper's grudging admission that the sale of these games to the 'underage' boys was not actually illegal was buried at the end of the report. What was perhaps most shocking about the whole exercise was the amount of time the two intrepid investigators wasted in going to the shops in person. Had they stayed at home in front of their computers, they could have ordered the games directly from the *Sun*'s own online mail order service – at least until the day after the story ran, when someone at the newspaper noticed this, and swiftly had it removed. By the August bank holiday, however, the paper had forgotten the danger posed by computer games, and were offering 'FREE' with the August 27 edition, the 'no-nonsense, butt-kicking', and extremely violent *Duke*

Nukem: Manhattan Project to every reader, as 'Something for the Weekend.'

Away from the entertaining hypocrisy of the media, 'serious' debate as to the dangers posed by video games was conducted. The psychologist Professor Mark Griffiths of Nottingham Trent University told BBC Radio Five Live that he 'felt a link had already been proved between violence and videogames in children aged eight years or below but more study was needed into the long-term impact of bloodthirsty games on the behaviour of older children.' Griffiths claimed that 'research has shown those aged eight years or below do in the short term re-enact or copy what they see on screen'.

While this may be true, to suggest that children re-enact everything that they see on screen is ridiculous. Most of the computer games or films that children see feature high speed car chases, intergalactic battles, talking ogres, flying witches and 'never-ending' stories as much as they do bloodthirsty humans. What they then do is *pretend* to enact what they see on screen. To suggest that this necessarily leads to their actually behaving like the fantastic characters on screen is absurd, not least because, for the most part, to do so would be impossible. Beyond the impossibility of children jumping onto broomsticks and taking to the skies for a relaxing game of Quidditch, the idea that they believe themselves to be the characters they inhabit is absurd, patronising, and fails to understand the nature of childish play. Children are perfectly aware that their games are, precisely that, games. If they thought that their enactment was real, how could they explain their friends getting up again when they are bored with being 'dead'?

An essential part of playing, be it such outdoor, physical games, or indoor computer games, is the ability to distinguish between the game and reality. Where children become obsessed and deluded into being unable to make that distinction, the fault usually lies with the parents who have not paid their children sufficient attention for them to know where reality ends and fantasy begins. To blame the computer games in such an incident is to abdicate parental responsibility.

Even if very impressionable children are influenced by violent films or computer games, the influence can only be one of the many thousands of contributing factors to their behaviour. To claim that such a small influence is the *cause* of their behaviour is a trifle unscientific. But such logic-chopping has its uses in that people making these arguments would easily show how their first conclusion is not invalidated by the fact that the vast majority of those who play games such as *Manhunt* or watch films such as *Child's Play 3* but don't go about murdering each other.

Naturally, however, in the aftermath of the Leblanc prosecution, there was talk of bringing corporate manslaughter charges against Rockstar Games, the manufacturers of *Manhunt*. The greatest absurdity was perhaps that, if the accused in the case had followed the same logic, he could possibly have expected to be acquitted, given that he was not finally responsible for the murder, *Manhunt* was. The crucial fact that must be remembered is that, terrible as the tragedy was, the poor boy killed in this senseless crime was killed by an insane teenager armed with the actual physical weapons of a knife and a claw hammer, not with a computer game.

Actual physical weapons produce an altogether more hysterical response from the media, the public and the government, however, as the reaction to the Dunblane massacre of 1996 demonstrated.

The events of Wednesday, March 13, 1996, were as horrific and as impossible to assimilate as any such mindless tragedy could be. Thomas Hamilton, a deranged and embittered ex-head of the Dunblane Rover's Group – a group similar in essence to the Boy Scouts – walked into the primary school of the small Scottish town, heavily armed, and embarked on an indiscriminate killing spree of a class in the gymnasium. After killing sixteen children, all between four and six years of age, and one adult teacher, Hamilton killed himself.

Any such tragedy devastates the families and the community involved, and the extent of its horror always leads to an angry call for justice, which, in the event of the murderer taking his own life, can never be administered. Instead, a scapegoat had to be found. The fault of the tragedy, inevitably, lay squarely at the door of the madman who had caused it. Without him, however, the directionless and insatiable anger found its scapegoat in the innocuous activities of gun clubs, one of which Hamilton had been a member.

With the consent of Bob Dylan, a Dunblane musician named Ted Christopher wrote a new verse for 'Knockin' On Heaven's Door' in memory of the children and their teacher. The recording of the revised version of the song, which included surviving school children singing in the chorus and Mark Knopfler on guitar, was released on December 9, 1996. The proceeds went to charities for children. The resultant heartstrings that were pulled led to a public outcry against the existence of guns and a government inquiry was held, led by Lord Cullen.

Taking into account that Hamilton possessed the firearms legally, this inquiry led to restrictions on handguns in the United Kingdom. Ironically this angered both the pro-gun lobby (who opposed any restrictions) and the anti-gun lobby (who felt the restrictions were too weak).

A nationwide amnesty was then declared, with all now-prohibited weapons having to be turned in to the police, and a Firearms Bill was hastily drafted and put through parliament which proposed to ban nearly two hundred thousand handguns of .22 calibre and over.

One of the most outspoken critics of the amnesty and the ban was the Duke of Edinburgh, who said in an interview with BBC Radio Five, 'I think one's got to make a difference between what the weapons can do and what the people can do. And there are always going to be unstable people who are going to do monstrous things. We know that but I don't think it helps by taking it out on the rest of the population.'

This entirely sensible point of view was seized on by the tabloid press and the anti-gun campaigners, particularly because he followed it with the analogy of cricket, 'If a cricketer, for instance, suddenly decided to go into a school and batter a lot of people to death with a cricket bat which he could do very easily, I mean, are you going to ban cricket bats?'

The Guardian-reading public were predictably outraged, but used his comments as an excuse to launch a childish attack on his character rather than to address his eminently sensible point. He could have been more tactful, perhaps, in his approach, but ultimately what he said was entirely reasonable. Banning guns because of the actions of one lunatic makes as much sense as banning cars because of one car crash. The Duke's comments were not as callous and insensitive as the media delighted in portraying them either, for he acknowledged the tragedy and respected the sufferings of its victims' families:

> I sympathise desperately with the people who are bereaved at Dunblane, but I'm not altogether convinced that it's the best system to somehow shift the blame on to a very large and peaceable part of the community, in a sense, in trying to make yourself feel better. I can't believe that members of shooting clubs are any more dangerous than members of a squash club or a golf club or anything else. I mean, they're perfectly reasonable people, like the great majority of people in this country.
>
> There are always going to be unstable people who are going to do monstrous things. But I don't think that it helps by taking it out on the rest of the population
>
> The new legislation would not prevent guns getting into the hands of the criminals – if it's illegal, it means you shouldn't be doing it. But you've got to police that. It's no good just saying you can't do it. You actually have to police it.

Despite, or perhaps because of, the almost unprecedented situation in which the most valuable and considered contribution to a national debate was offered by a member of the Royal Family, the ban went into almost immediate effect.

The only real effect of the gun control laws introduced after Dunblane, other than infuriating the members of gun clubs and the British Olympic Shooting team (one of whose members, Richard Faulds, won Britain's second gold in the Sydney 2000 games, despite his sport's vilification by the anti-gun lobby), was to increase the State's control over law-abiding members of society.

For non law-abiding members of society, however, access to guns has become easier, as the fact that firearms offences are reported to have doubled would indicate. When four teenage girls were shot at a New Year party in a hairdresser's in Birmingham in 2004, two of whom were killed, the police described the shootings as 'exceptional in their brutality' and 'unprecedented'. The Home Office immediately announced a top-level summit to organise an emergency crackdown on Britain's 'gun culture'.

How, given the crack-down on weapons in the wake of the Dunblane tragedy, such a 'gun culture' had developed in which 'unprecedented' crimes could take place was not explained. However, it was announced that the government would be instigating a 'crackdown' on replica weapons and airguns. Also, police chiefs promised to target such evils as 'gangsta' rap music, violent video games, and other aspects of 'teen culture'. Like the hoodlums who killed the two girls in Birmingham, however, such irrelevant measures showed that the government is only tough enough to shoot at easy targets. Instead of accepting that the real problems are immensely difficult to understand and are underpinned by complex social and economic factors, they pretend that such tragedies can casually be blamed on a comparatively innocuous 'teen culture' and eradicated with a few pieces of legislation directed at record companies and the manufacturers of computer games.

Perhaps the tragedy which has most mobilised the public and media's outrage in recent years was the murder of the two Cambridgeshire schoolgirls, Jessica Chapman and Holly Wells, in August 2002. Almost more so than the tragedy at Dunblane, the story of the two girls was wrested from the hands of the relevant authorities by the newspapers, who made the entire case, with all its failings, their own. Acting together, the various media outlets that gave blanket coverage to the unfolding of the girls' disappearance, discovery and the piecing together of what had happened to them, could have pretty much pushed the story in which ever direction they wished, as was shown by the universal hatred subsequently shown by members of the public for Maxine Carr who, for all her abysmal failings, crimes, and dishonesty, was found to have had nothing to do with the abduction and murder of the two girls.

Naturally, a scapegoat was found for the case: this time, the failure of the government agencies that allowed Ian Huntley to be employed as a caretaker by the school, with recommendations that, in future, there be much tighter vetting of those who work with children. Of course, those that work closely with children must be proven fit to do so, but taking into account allegations made against a prospective employee, rather than charges or convictions, means that countless applicants for jobs could be prejudiced against merely because a wrongful accusation had been made against them in the past.

Furthermore, the change in the system would only close the *exact* loophole that had allowed Huntley's employment. In fact, children in future would still be vulnerable to the attacks of violent paedophiles such as Huntley, they would just have to find another way of getting access to them. In the meantime, Britain would have been pushed that bit closer to the rejection of the basic judicial principle of the presumption of innocence.

The fact that, if a crime so horrible as Huntley's does happen again in this country it will doubtless cause equal uproar, demonstrates that such crimes become notorious precisely because they are so rare. Child murder and paedophilia have become such a national obsession because of their enormous ability to shock, which is inversely related to their frequency. Judging by reports in the media, however, one could be forgiven for assuming that every other unmarried man is prone to extreme sexual perversion, and that one in five owners of computers use them primarily for looking at children in sexually compromising poses on the internet.

On March 7th, 2004, a photographic exhibition exploring childhood was launched at the Spitz Gallery in London as part of a festival of women's writing. One of the exhibitions was by an American artist called Betsy Schneider, and showed naked pictures of her daughter between birth and the age of five. Such a harmless exhibition immediately captured the attention of the media, who decided that the Spitz Gallery was guilty of displaying child pornography. It was reported that Scotland Yard had been called and the police had been dispatched. Unable to decide whether or not the pictures were actually 'obscene', the police recommended the closure of the gallery while lawyers were consulted.

The lunacy of the allegedly 'paedophilic' images being so innocuous that the police themselves were unable to decide whether or not they were pornographic should have been obvious. However, it was not, and *The Sun* was 'reluctantly' forced, to demonstrate its point, to reprint one of the obscene, child-threatening pictures alongside a 'genuine' picture taken from a 'child porn website'. When viewed side by side, the paper claimed that the two pictures demonstrated that 'the difference between art and child pornography is NIL.' How *The Sun* managed legally to obtain the picture from the child porn website was not revealed. Nor was the percentage of the paper's three million strong readership who used the picture to exercise anything other than their moral outrage.

Clearly, however, the Nanny State could not ignore this and similar hype, and, in May 2002, surrounded by even more hype, 'Operation Ore' was launched, with more than 3,200 raids resulting in 723 suspects being charged, and 227 convicted.

While there is a chance that this operation succeeded in preempting attacks on children, it also brought the whole complicated subject of paedophilia into the mainstream media forever. And, as with anything where the chief development of policy is decided on the pages of the tabloids, the result was chaos. So much so that nobody seems prepared to accept that there is a difference between those who have naughty thoughts involving children and those that actually go into playgrounds and attempt to abuse them. There is, obviously, an enormous difference, but one which the suggested legislation refuses to acknowledge.

Tink Palmer, the principal policy officer at the children's charity Barnardo's, has claimed that 'if every person who had a sexual interest in children was identified...I think you would be amazed.'

Beyond the fact that this means Palmer somehow has possession of a statistic that is impossible to acquire, it demonstrates the alarmist thinking behind the scaremongering Nanny State. The most abhorrent of the proposed legislation in reaction to this was that suggested by the Lord Chief Justice, Lord Woolf in December 2001, who recommended that suspected paedophiles should be put in prison before they committed any crime. This mammoth tipping of the balance in favour of security over liberty is vile in the extreme, but was only rejected by David Blunkett on the grounds that it would not work in practice. It would also have caused chaos at the Department of Work and Pensions, where, in the first eight months of 2004, an investigation revealed that civil servants had looked at 2,319,569 pornographic images, many of which involved children.

Of all the 'hobgoblins' with which the government has been able to menace the public, the one that has proven even more effective in allowing the enforcement of the Nanny State than the lurking threat of paedophilia, was provided by the events of 11 September, 2001.

Obviously, there can never be any excuse made for the actions of the hijackers on that day, but this does not excuse the behaviour of the legislature in the attacks' wake. The idiotic but persistent pronouncements of Blair and other members of the government that an attack on British soil is not a question of 'if but when', should demonstrate nothing more than this government's acceptance of its own incompetence. However, keeping the public terrified of such imminent danger has two advantages. First, it provides a justification for Blair's expensive and questionable foreign expeditions and, second, it gives a premise for the Nanny State to dream up raft after raft of exciting new means to rid the public of their freedoms.

Privacy may strike most people as a particularly vital freedom. As far as the Nanny State is concerned, however, it is a downright nuisance. Like the child not allowed to lock the bathroom door 'in case something happens', the public are being scrutinised with increasing frequency and invasiveness by the state. The conviction that the government is watching your every move, scientifically monitoring your very existence, has long been the preserve of lonely conspiracy theorists and paranoid hippies. In a gesture of inclusiveness, however, the Nanny State has generously extended this creepy discomfort to the entire nation.

'Justified' by the increased risk of terrorism, the government's top-secret GCHQ has evaluated new biometric technology that identifies people by body odour. The Home Office is convinced that 'identity' is a pressing problem in counter-terrorism enforcement, despite the fact that the majority of the 9/11 hijackers used their real names. More significantly, none of the Madrid train bombers could have been apprehended in a preemptive strike on bogus aliases because they all had valid ID cards. Nevertheless, greater efficiency in checking identities is believed to be vital in the war on terror.

The Department of Trade and Industry recently listed 'identity theft' as the fastest-growing type of crime, and have decided that 'biometrics' are the solution. A spokesman for the Government agency Qinetiq bragged:

> ...it may sound completely ridiculous, but it's a fantastic
> way of identifying people. It's almost impossible to fake or

duplicate someone's own personal pong. It's certainly a lot
more efficient than everyone trying to remember dozens of
PIN numbers, and no one is going to force you at knife-
point to divulge the secrets of your body odour to let them
withdraw money from your cashpoint!'

Muggers do not tend to ask for your cashcard and PIN number.
They usually march you to a cashpoint and make you withdraw the
money yourself. Arguably, the method of withdrawal would make no
difference whatsoever to them. Their only concern would be that their
victims' smell of fear temporarily masked their customary scent.
Furthermore, making ID cards compulsory is a fairly extreme
measure to combat cashpoint crime. The Home Office are making far
greater claims than Qinetiq itself, however, and intend to use
biometrics to fight terrorism, immigration and benefit fraud.

Use of the new technology will be reliant on every citizen of the
United Kingdom possessing a 'security card'. The use of such cards,
according to Blunkett, '...will make identity theft and multiple
identity impossible – not nearly impossible, impossible'. It is unclear
how Blunkett would deal with the presumably still-relevant problem
of card theft, however.

He also fails to mention the problem of people gaining a card
under a false identity in the first place. The Home Secretary has
conceded, somewhat unwillingly, that ID cards will not help combat
this crime. Indeed, they will likely to make it more prevalent as
criminals or terrorists have to find new ways of evading detection.
Furthermore, the cards' developers have advised government officials
not to use the technology for their own use in checking and

identifying Whitehall staff because it might not work properly. Doubts over the cards' efficiency are leading experts to advise a three-year wait before putting them to 'official' use. The card is good enough for us, however, and ten thousand citizens are already being monitored as they 'sample' the card. Mark Oaten, Liberal Democrat Shadow Home Secretary, voiced the concerns of many MPs when he said that the Home Office has '...put the cart before the horse in pretending that it can build a £3bn system on the back of technology which is still in development'.

The sad truth is that such pretences are commonplace with New Labour, but the desire to monitor each of us with deadly scientific accuracy to 'control immigration' misses the point entirely. A coherent policy in the first place would be a far better way to tackle the issue, the main fault of which is not 'bogus' asylum-seekers in any case. It is not just coherent policy which is lacking, however. The raft of distinct problems which ID cards are intended to 'solve' are so numerous that the new technology ends up looking like a handy catch-all tool of little specific or practical value.

It does make the population feel uncomfortable, however, as it highlights the government's contemptuous attitude towards the citizen. We are all potential criminals who cannot be trusted when we say who we are, and must therefore be monitored by the state. ID cards are a particularly dramatic example of the government's general habit of combating a tiny minority of wrongdoers by treating everybody like criminals. The only people who cannot object to this, in fact, are criminals and terrorists. Genuine al-Qaeda operatives will never be stupid enough to complain that their civil liberties are being eroded. They will simply go along to the nearest Post Office, quietly have their photo taken, receive their terrorist-battling ID card and then go home to keep plotting. But Blunkett is impervious to criticism:

> I happen to believe that, once we get this up and running,
> people will queue up for it and we will have to deal with a
> flow and a flood of people wanting it much earlier, wanting
> to renew their passport to get an ID card very fast.

This is despite the fact that the technology simply does not work. A leaked GCHQ document warned of 'a series of hardware, software and ergonomic problems leading to inconsistent enrolment.' What may simply be 'inconsistent enrolment' for the government would be a nightmare for an individual denied access to his basic civil and human rights by faulty technology. The government is nevertheless keen to press ahead despite these problems, with Blunkett warning, '...people better get their identity pretty quickly otherwise they are going to find themselves in a real mess to establish a real identity for life'. What does he mean? Quite apart from the fact that the search for our identity has been at the centre of philosophical thought for centuries, he is insistent that a half-baked system riddled with errors will be infallible.

What is worse is that our civil liberties are being eroded pointlessly. Brian Hadfield, managing director of Unisys, who has worked on ID card schemes in South Africa and Malaysia, has serious doubts about their usefulness: 'An ID card is best equipped to handle things like fraud, and has the capability to minimise exposure to credit-card and welfare fraud, but I don't think it would have a huge impact on security and terrorism.' This is a serious flaw in the scheme, given its entire raison d'etre, and its projected cost of over £3 bn. A Liberal Democrat statement summed up the likely reality:

> ...it has all the hallmarks of a disaster waiting to happen. No one has spelt out what the cards are for or how they will achieve their objectives. Building the system is complex and massively expensive, the cost estimates are vague and incomplete, and the project is reliant on new and untested technology.

Previous government schemes to 'reform' the Passport Service and the Child Support Agency have gone massively over-budget, reinforcing the doubts about the ID card scheme. Gathering information for a database capable of storing the details of every UK resident will be almost impossible, and will be instantly out of date. The fact that hundreds of thousands of people a year change their address in London alone is compounded by minor issues like name change through marriage. Hadfield himself, who should know, says:

> ...from day one it will be almost out of date. As with many programmes, you can work out how much it costs to set up, but it will cost a lot more to maintain its accuracy...it will be a monumental project.

Given New Labour's data-maintenance track record, the possibility of disaster is daunting. It is obvious to those not desperate for quickfire solutions to difficult problems that biometric technology will not even be very effective with tens of millions of people, because the differences between each measurement in the database will shrink with each person added. The aim cannot hope to justify the cost, either. Malaysia's Unisys manager, Lalit Gupta, points out the card's limitations:

> The card is very easy to validate who is a Malaysian and who is not. What it does not do is to help identify non-Malaysians who are involved in wrong activity. That would require different solutions.'

Even Blunkett has been forced to concede that most terrorists use their own identity, although he still insists that countries without biometric security '...will be known to the terrorists to be the easiest touch'. The exact opposite is more likely to be true. Professor Martyn Thomas, of the UK Computing Research Committee, said in February 2004, 'You are adding to the nation's critical infrastructure unnecessarily and by doing that, you are making a very large range of services, probably a growing range of services, vulnerable to a single attack.' US civil liberties group Electronic Frontier Foundation go further, saying that '...sorting out the vanishingly small minority of actual terrorists from the millions of "good guys" in an ID system will never be accomplished by an ID system, but rather through good police and intelligence work'.

David Davis has fumed that '...if this was really the answer to terrorism, the government would do it a hell of a lot sooner than 2012'. Not carrying one's card will not in itself be an offence, either, as long as a card is presented to a police station within three working days. 'In the case of a hardened terrorist, I doubt they would bother,' he surmised. This is lost on the British government, though, who are all-too-conscious of the friends to be made in the world of IT big-business by spending all our money on such a hopeless and unnecessary scheme.

The scheme here will target those who tend to be most law-abiding, as those who don't work, drive, vote or hold British passports will not be required to carry them until after 2013. Presuming that your average terrorist, particularly if in the country illegally, doesn't bother to vote, work or have a valid driving licence, he does not even number amongst those that qualify for the scheme. Given that terrorism prevention is the main reason the population are prepared to countenance ID cards, this seems self-defeating. It is worryingly easy to envisage a future in which law-abiding citizens are regularly stopped and asked to present their ID cards while terrorists commit atrocities in anonymity. In the awful eventuality of Britain suffering an attack before 2013, the culprits are most likely not to be legally obliged to possess ID cards. The police, however, will have even less time to hunt for them, as they will be so tied up with analysing the documentation of those who do not wish the country any harm The most ridiculous aspect of such a scenario is its plausibility.

The sense that the wrong people are being not just watched but actually persecuted will be intensified by ID cards. Ordinary citizens will be obliged to entrust all the information about themselves in police, tax, social security and NHS databases to a system they will have no right to access. Ironically, the country would probably be safer if everyone did have access to it. Family, friends and neighbours are far more likely to spot inconsistencies or inaccuracies in someone's details than a database monitored by strangers. Clearly, it would be most peoples' idea of a nightmare to let the general public know about their embarrassing operations or shameful convictions, but is it worse than being forced to give all such information to a faceless system? At least a public system can be publically monitored. A corrupt civil servant, on the other hand, could sell sensitive health information about somebody to a newspaper in complete anonymity.

Both systems have hideous problems attendant upon them because they are alternate versions of a rotten idea. Identity cards 'fail every practical and principled measure', according to Liberty, and are the requirement of a government demanding the trust of an electorate it doesn't trust in turn. Taking the condemnation further even than Liberty was Richard Thomas, the Information Commissioner, head of an independent body and answerable to Parliament. In August 2004 he singled out three projects that he believed posed a serious threat to the freedom of the citizen, chief among them was Blunkett's beloved ID card scheme:

> My anxiety is that we don't sleepwalk into a surveillance society where much more information is collected about people, accessible to far more people shared across many more boundaries than British Society would feel comfortable with. The Government has changed its line over the last two or three years as to what the card is intended for. You have to have clarity. Is it for the fight against terrorism? Is it to promote immigration control? Is it to provide access to public benefit and services?

He could equally have asked, 'Is it to serve any useful function whatsoever?'

If we were relinquishing our civil liberties in the name of actual progress, there would at least be a positive side to the process. The government's obsession with data-collection and statistics, however, does not even result in greater efficiency. The so-called 'knowledge economy' is exceptionally expensive, even for an administration spending enormous sums thoughtlessly the whole time, and criminal records are shambolically badly organised. It seems reasonable to assume that the transfer of criminal records to a database is the entire point of protective data collection. A suspect's criminal history should be accessible through a responsibly managed police system, so that employers are able, for example, to weed out paedophiles who want to work with children at an early stage. Grimsby authorities' mismanagement of information about Ian Huntley's history, for instance, highlights the flaws in the current system, but government reform proposals would make things worse. The fact that Cambridgeshire Police did not know about Huntley's past is terrible, but he had never been tried for his crimes before, let alone convicted. Knowledge of his behaviour towards underage girls in Hull would have been crucially important both to Soham school authorities and the police, but because he had never actually been charged, they had no way of accessing this information. It is not going too far to suggest that this led directly to the deaths of Holly Wells and Jessica Chapman. Neither is it going too far to suggest, however, that Ian Huntley was an extremely dangerous man not comparable to the vast majority of society. If we respond to his crimes by making it compulsory for separate authorities to share information regardless of evidence, large numbers of falsely accused people will have their lives ruined and it will not stop children being murdered.

You only need to look at the enthusiasm with which the tabloids reported that Massive Attack's Robert del Naja had been arrested for paedophilia and had the hard drive of his computer confiscated to see how invidious such a system would be. The media were entirely at liberty to report that the rock star was a sick pervert who didn't deserve to live amongst decent people. They were also entirely at liberty not to report a few days later that the innocent del Naja was the victim of a jealous ex-girlfriend who had telephoned Bristol Police and lied about what they would find on the star's computer. Del Naja was unlucky enough to be of sufficient public interest for the national media to report his tribulations, despite the fact that he had done nothing wrong. He is also famous enough, however, for news of his innocence to fight through the media's subsequent lack of interest in his reputation.

Those without the dubious benefits of fame, however, would find themselves at the mercy of anybody prepared to lie about them, and the authorities would have no choice but to pass on the useless but extremely damaging information to anyone who asked for it. If two people were competing for the same job, one would only need to invent a criminal story about the other and call the police with it to guarantee that the job was theirs. Even worse than this is Blunkett's determination to apply the legislation retrospectively. Thus the unfortunate Chief Constable David Westwood in Hull was personally and virtually illegally fired by the Home Secretary himself for a 'crime' which he genuinely had not committed. Indeed, at the time of Huntley's move from Humberside to Soham, it would have been unethical and possibly against the law for the hapless chief constable to inform Cambridgeshire Police of their new resident's history of unsubstantiated allegations. Upsettingly, in Huntley's extremely unusual case the information would have been incredibly useful, but to legislate on the basis that everyone might be as evil as he is would upset the balance of trust that is necessary within society.

Tony Blair himself has often boasted of the unprecedented levels of security and safety new technology can give us. It is dismaying to learn, therefore, that a recent audit by the Metropolitan Police found that eighty per cent of its records on the Police National Computer contained errors. Blair's dreams for a 'civil society' are directly reliant on technology that is wrong four times out of five. A concurrent survey reported that the percentage of convictions entered on the Police National Computer within a month of the trial was zero. Such incompetence suggests that the PNC does not even qualify as an elementary data bank, but rather than improve it, the government have simply appointed Capita, perhaps the worst private company in Whitehall, to take over the task. Capita are intent on unmasking potential child abusers, but are so incompetent at vetting teachers that they have kept schools closed rather than expose innocent children to those they have yet to 'assess'.

The message to teachers nationwide is that they are all potential paedophiles until cleared by Capita. Equally, the message to paedophiles is that if they can fool Capita, they can proceed with impunity. When the government vow to 'cut red tape' and 'get more bobbies on the beat' what they actually mean is that they will cut basic record-keeping and deny the police vital information which might lead them to suspects.

Scaremongering is a vital political tool for this government because it inhibits people from responding rationally to proposed legislation. No one likes living in fear, and we are therefore inclined to let the government do whatever it likes to make us feel safe and happy again. If you actually look at the 'facts', however, they start to disappear like little puffs of smoke.

Do B-movies make children kill each other? No, but it is easier to ban *Child's Play Three: Chucky's Revenge* than it would be to address the cycles of deprivation, violence and despair in which children behave like savages.

Was the video game *Manhunt* responsible for the death of Stefan Pakeerah? No, Warren Leblanc was, but it is far easier to sell newspapers in which MPs fulminate against toys as if they are 'child pornography' than it is to sell them by reporting that a disturbed adolescent stabbed someone.

Will ID cards stop a 9/11-style atrocity happening here? Of course not, but it is much easier to pretend that an expensive but unworkable new system will prevent terrorist attacks than it is to promote the genuine understanding and integration which will ultimately deny terrorists a breeding ground in this country.

Does the Nanny State solve any of the problems our society faces? No, but it is much easier to pretend that it does than to admit that it doesn't.

5 There, there, it's not your fault...

I want that glib and oily art, to speak and purpose not.

William Shakespeare, *King Lear*

In early 1998, Tony Blair gave an interview to his favourite bastion of morality, *The Sun*. During the course of a characteristically meaningless exposition of his political philosophy, he stated, '...Britons need to stop wringing their hands and start taking more responsibility for their own lives.' This was tough talk from a no-nonsense Prime Minister, undoubtedly; but it seemed somewhat at odds with his own Third Way manifesto. Later the same year, Andrew Giddens, author of *The Third Way,* told *The Guardian,* '...the overall aim of Third Way politics should be to help citizens plot their way through the major revolutions of our time: globalisation, transformations in personal life and our relationship to nature.'

What was the British public to make of this? The Prime Minister was telling them to 'stop wringing their hands and start taking more responsibility for their own lives' and yet the author of his own favourite book was defining 'New' Labour's aim as 'to help citizens' attempting to cope with 'transformations in their personal life'. To make matters even more confusing, Blair himself was a hand-wringer *par excellence*. In August, 1997, he had held hands with the entire nation during his speech following the death of Princess Diana. He said that:

> I feel like everyone else in the country today. We are today a nation, in Britain, in a state of shock, in mourning, in grief that is so deeply painful for us.

The untimely death of the princess inevitably induced powerful feelings of shock and grief in people. Those people, however, were her sons, family, friends, close acquaintances and the various tabloid editors who could genuinely claim to have lost something through her passing. As for the assorted nutcases that flooded to the gates of Kensington Palace preposterously claiming to have lost something equally personal through her death, what was needed was not the sanctioning of their insanity by the Prime Minister, but a short, sharp reality check. Blair, presumably possessed of some intelligence, must have been well aware of this, but instead chose to exploit the situation, not to mention the genuine grief of the princess's family, for his own political gain. The fact that he was blinking back tears as he spoke added to the effect. He may have been running the country, but he also felt like everyone else, stricken by a 'grief that is so deeply painful for us'. Throughout the address, he was visibly wringing his hands, doubtless at the thought of all the political capital he was going to make out of her death.

The inevitable result of Blair's leadership style is that Britain is increasingly in the grip of professionally qualified, publicly funded counsellors. Napoleon's disparaging description of England as a 'nation of shopkeepers' has been re-formulated for a new millennium – we are now a nation of therapists. The number of mental health professionals has more than quadrupled since 1970, but even more significant is that the ranks of registered psychotherapists swelled by more than half between 1997 and 1999. Demand is inevitably keeping pace with supply, and it is becoming increasingly difficult to watch a television programme that doesn't end by encouraging viewers to pick up the phone 'if you have been affected by any of the issues raised in the course of this programme'. The implication is that every difficult experience requires expert help, and people are encouraged to feel traumatised and depressed by events hitherto regarded as routine. We have not been rendered emotionally crippled under New Labour, but the 'therapeutic ethos' does soften us up to the government's message.

The result of this is clear, and has potentially catastrophic consequences for future generations: people are becoming so accustomed to Nanny's fussing over them that many are becoming almost incapable of existence without the knowledge that her comforting shoulder is always there to cry on.

For the state, this has two significant rewards. First, it creates a nation of dependents for whom voting the government out of office would be the electoral equivalent of a child throwing away its beloved 'blanky'. Second, it opens up an enormous market for the usual collection of otherwise unemployable misfits to quickly claim 'expertise' in whichever invented field of pseudo-science best addresses the latest craze and, then, enrol themselves in a highly paid and easy job as its 'counsellor'.

Of course there are emotional difficulties in life for which the best remedy is open discussion with another person. Traditionally, however, such intangible human emotions as grief, insecurity, trauma and the rest have been coped with alone or with the support of trusted friends and family. The idea that some half-educated stranger can help tackle the most complex, personal and particular anguish of a person's life with some half-baked, catch-all 'formula' of grief-counselling is as patronising and as ridiculous as the government's other ludicrous idea that parenting, an equally individual and idiosyncratic discipline, can be boiled down to a few easy lessons and 'taught' by an outsider. However, the inexorable rise in the number of such pointlessly occupied civil-servants continues, and their pernicious influence is creeping into every aspect of civilised life. A study published in *New Scientist* in November 2003 showed that counselling victims of traumatic events generally do more harm than good and, rather than having any positive effect, can actually hinder natural recovery. Naturally, however, no attention was paid to such a anti-Nanny finding.

In February 2004, Ruth Beddows, a supply teacher from the sleepy village of Murcott in Oxfordshire, was the victim of a rare criminal adventure for that part of the country: somebody broke into her garden shed and stole her lawnmower. On discovery of the break-in she rang the police and told them of the crime, rather vainly hoping that she might retrieve the mower, as she was due to host the local Women's Institute meeting that weekend and had hoped to serve cool glasses of Pimm's to the members on a freshly mown lawn. Later that day, no fewer than three police officers were dispatched to the village from Oxford – the city in which the nearest police station was based. On arrival they informed her that there was nothing they could do to return the lawnmower, however, they had some good news – they were able to put her in touch with a counsellor to help her come to terms with the loss... her lawnmower!

Miss Beddows thanked them warmly for the offer while quickly showing them the door. But other country-folk, still trying to make sense of their urban counterparts' cloth-headed failure to understand man's natural relationship to animals, might have pursued a less polite course of action and laughed openly at the latest absurdity of the pampered 'townies' and the divorce from reality that is the result of their cocooned and insular lives. No longer, as this 'coddling' of individuals has already spread into rural Britain, as was highlighted by the Foot and Mouth outbreak of 2001. Such a crisis, inevitably a political minefield, and handled badly by the government, was good news for urban mental health organisations, who were able to exploit distraught farmers. The Rural Stress Information Service (which didn't exist during the far worse Foot and Mouth outbreak of 1967) reported a tenfold increase in calls to its helpline, with some callers 'breaking down in tears'.

The enthusiasm with which government information agencies

spread 'awareness' of newly-discovered psychological conditions becomes an exercise in discovering sufferers from the particular trauma of the day. *Woman's Hour* unquestioningly announced in 2002 that '...one in five young people rates stress as unbearably high most of the time'. The programme attempted to highlight the urgent need for more state investment in counselling services. The presenter, Jenni Murray, considered the statistic itself inviolable, because it was 'backed up by a number of government organisations'. Adrienne Katz, chief executive of the charity Young Voice, was brought in to explain that primary school children are becoming hugely stressed at the prospect of moving into the senior school. Given that this move has been carried out for over a century by millions of children, usually with great delight at no being longer an infant, it is likely that the root cause of their 'huge stress' is not the move itself. A more likely stress creator can be located in people like Adrienne Katz. It is possibly unwise to broadcast on primetime radio the idea that children are 'hugely stressed' by something as potentially positive and exciting as the graduation to senior school.

Children are obviously the most impressionable section of society, and are quite capable of describing themselves as 'hugely stressed' without appreciating what it really means. The chances of them doing so are greatly increased in an environment where adults are definitively declaring them to be so.

We learn how to be adults in stages, the first of which is to copy grown-ups unquestioningly. This manifests itself in the very young as an exact physical mimicry of a parent. The scene in Spielberg's *Jaws* where Sheriff Brody wearily rubs his eyes and sips his coffee at the kitchen table as his infant son sits opposite attempting to mimic him is a perfect example of this. The child doesn't raise his pudgy hands to his face because he too is tired, and nor does he suck at his bottle of milk to give himself a much-needed caffeine boost. He is simply trying to be like his daddy. As children grow, they copy language as well as movement, which is, fairly obviously, how they develop their vocabulary. They also start trying to feel like adults by copying adult speech patterns and trying to emulate adult concerns. This is the context in which the 'huge stress' of moving to big school should be understood. If children claim to be so worried, it is because they are receptacles for the stress and tension adults project on to them. Adrienne Katz could have seized her fifteen minutes on *Woman's Hour* to talk about how great senior school can be, but instead she chose to create a self-fulfilling prophecy. You can almost imagine carefree children playing as their mothers listen to *Woman's Hour* and pricking up their ears as something relevant to their own lives is introduced. Within seconds, My Little Ponies and Action Men are discarded as children everywhere think to themselves, 'Yes. I *am* hugely stressed about the move to my next school. Mummy, what does 'stressed' mean?'

Katz also added that bullying and racism had increased as a result of 9/11 2001. The primary solution proposed by organisations like Young Voice, however, was to counsel the victims rather than to educate or punish the bullies and racists. The BBC was presenting an image of social responsibility, but all it was really doing was cultivating a deeply unhealthy sense of therapeutic anxiety. Frank Furedi, a professor of Sociology at the University of Kent, summed up the way this works in his book, *Therapy Culture*:

> ...the crucial characteristic of all therapy culture is its
> manipulative ambition. The belief that there is a fairly
> narrow range of 'appropriate' emotions for each situation
> carries with it an obligation to produce those emotions.
> School life, family policy, employment practice and the
> justice system must all be redesigned to minimise the
> danger of causing hurt or offence.

Perhaps it would be 'offensive' to school bullies to object to their racism in the playground. Instead, bullied children are subjected to both the pain of victimisation and the humiliation of being identified as a victim. The innumerable healthier and more effective ways of dealing with bullying are discarded in favour of this method. The real worry is that no one seems to question the wisdom of subjecting huge numbers of people, particularly children, to therapy. As Furedi points out, '...training a child how to feel is a far more intrusive and coercive process than educating a pupil how to behave'.

It is not just children being trained how to feel, either. In his speech at the Labour Party conference in 2000, Blair needed to show his 'feelings' to counteract the immense bad publicity caused by the recent petrol price crisis. He spoke of being 'torn' as he attempted to listen to the public and 'do the right thing'. He appeared unaware of the offensiveness of suggesting that the two were incompatible, merely stating that he could not pursue a policy if '...I know in my heart it's not right'. The conference was closely followed by a series of adverts on television 'thanking' the nation for taking the responsibility for initiating change by voting for New Labour. There was no point whatsoever to the adverts, except to boost national self-esteem and make everyone feel better disposed towards the government. Subliminally, however, the short films were making the rather more sinister point that the government was not prepared to accept responsibility for its own policies except in partnership with those who had voted for it. Superficial emotionalism was not confined to ad breaks in *Big Brother*, however. Ten Downing Street's own website revealed New Labour's enthusiasm for formulating policy on the basis of how we feel, asking visitors: 'What actions do you think the government could take to make women feel more valued and respected in their roles as mothers, carers and active participants in their communities?'

On close inspection, the question is meaningless. How could you possibly legislate to make 'carers' feel 'valued' and 'respected' in ways which wold have any legal effect? Even if such legislation were possible, was the public seriously expected to believe that *it* could create new laws via a website? The question remained academic, however. Visitors found that any attempt to write something political, let alone critical or antagonistic, on the message board was futile. Unless comments were happy, positive and, frankly, legislatively useless, they were ignored in the final summation. The government computer was making its position very clear – only nice, encouraging suggestions were acknowledged. Inadvertently, this revealed the Government's contemptuous attitude towards the entire electorate.

It is only beneficial to the government to find out how we feel if we tell it we are feeling good, because then it is under no pressure to do anything. Unfortunately for New Labour, it is sometimes impossible to pretend that all is well. Such was the case at Middlesborough General Hospital in 2002 when twenty-four people were deemed to have been exposed to a theoretical risk of Creutzfeld-Jakob Disease (CJD).

Officials in the Department of Health reacted to the highly remote possibility that CJD had been transmitted to these people in a somewhat surprising manner. Rather than attempting to ascertain the probability of transmission or, even ,establishing how it had occurred, it despatched a team of counsellors to visit the 'victims'. The counsellors offered them support ('lifelong if necessary') to help them cope with the realisation that they might – but most probably would not – succumb to the symptoms of this untreatable neuro-degenerative disorder at some point in the future. It is conceivable that the twenty-four people in question would have found these government-sponsored harbingers of doom profoundly depressing, if not actively unhelpful. Given the remoteness of the risk, coupled with its untreatability in any event, the arrival of a team of strangers forcing them to contemplate their possible descent into madness and death in the name of 'counselling' could be deemed insensitive. At the very least, it might have been worth discovering whether the counsellors were wanted. Instead, twenty-four active citizens were shown that the government intended to treat them as victims in perpetuity. One 'victim' said, '...I was feeling pretty positive about the whole thing until this lot turned up, now I can't stop thinking about it and I'm really worried about the future.'

The government's need to show authority and concern was exemplified by Tony Blair's claim that the twenty-four hour telephone helpline NHS Direct was '...among the greatest achievements of my first term'. In reality, NHS Direct merely provided a symbolic link between needy individuals and a government desperate to show 'support' at every available opportunity. The 'support' itself did not carry with it any commitment to provide resources or services, but gave an impression of activity and social improvement. After all, it is much easier to despatch counsellors to help people deal with their problems than it is to tackle those problems.

Unfortunately, such an approach is worse than simply useless, as has been already referred to, there is a growing body of research indicates that counselling after distressing situations often has a harmful effect on individuals whose own coping strategies are undermined. An uncritical attitude towards modern psychosocial theories also tends to over-estimate demand. This is particularly obvious when applied to war victims. A recent survey by Medecins Sans Frontieres concluded that ninety-nine per cent of the population of Sierra Leone was suffering from severe Post Traumatic Stress Disorder (PTSD). This statistic is of very little practical value. It cannot seriously imply that ninety-nine per cent of Sierra Leone's population want counselling, nor can it be implying that one per cent of its population remained unaffected. Furthermore, if ninety nine per cent of the country's population started a course of counselling, a new survey would rapidly report that one per cent of the population of Sierra Leone were now feeling slighted and ignored. Psychiatrist

Derek Summerfield injected a note of sanity in his comment that there was a 'large over-estimate of the number of those needing treatment'.

The need to remain active and effective in the face of difficulties is obviously universal, but whereas in the past there has been an assumption that society consists of robust and resilient individuals, a minority of whom are susceptible to psychological disorders, New Labour's approach assumes universal vulnerability. This is the same government whose leader is obsessed with 'individual responsibility' and people looking after themselves. But the realisation that universal vulnerability is politically useful – even if it does diminish our autonomy as rational individuals – is too tempting for Blairites to resist. A denial of people's capacity to act as responsible citizens has consequences not only domestically, but also internationally. Vanessa Pupavac, a lecturer at Nottingham University, observed that:

> ...effectively, the psychosocial model involves both invalidation of the population's psychological responses and their invalidation as political actors, while validating the role of external actors. An indefinite suspension of self-government in post-conflict societies or so-called 'failed states' becomes thereby legitimised.

In other words, the Nanny State is not shy when it comes to applying its theories in places as dissimilar to England as Afghanistan or Iraq.

In June, 2004, Foreign Secretary Jack Straw backed a plan for psychologists to work with Afghan men who have trouble discussing their 'emotional problems', as part of a wider New Labour policy to give a higher priority to 'gender issues'. A Foreign Office report, entitled 'Inclusive Government: Mainstreaming Gender Into Foreign Policy' leaked by the *Mail on Sunday* on 13 June 2004, outlined the government's proposal to help the citizens of a country torn apart by war, chronic poverty, land mines, and the mass production of heroin:

> ...our policy in Afghanistan is to address the problems which men face and which are specific to their gender and traditional role. These include stigma against discussing 'emotional' problems. The patriarchal Afghan society does not encourage men to acknowledge or talk through difficult issues. This can mean they repress their problems and deal with them in inappropriate or antisocial ways.
>
> Our general strategy in Afghanistan promotes the establishment of professional counselling services, the development of a Department of Psychiatry at Kabul University and the provision of psychological training for doctors and hospital staff.

It also contained advice for ensuring that the publicity material distributed to the bewildered Afghans is suitably sensitive:

> Check that pictures in publicity material are not overwhelmingly of one sex, except where this is unavoidable, for example in a booklet about women's rights. Even then, a balanced view is better! And make sure that language is inclusive.

In response, Shadow Foreign Secretary Michael Ancram, said:

> I am all for sensible steps to remove discrimination and to

remove inequalities. However this booklet makes a mockery of the good work of the Foreign Office. In Afghanistan, where security and the restoration of democracy are paramount, the creation of a nanny state as suggested in this booklet is laughable. The Foreign Office should spend money on more important things.

A Foreign Office spokesman defended the counselling project, however, saying that 'there is a serious problem of men facing rapid change in society, becoming violent because they cannot cope', before adding, almost inevitably, 'there is also a serious issue of post-traumatic stress disorder facing many Afghans'.

The idea that the beliefs of the Nanny State should be exported to nations who never voted for this government nor, one can presume, would ever dream of doing so, is extraordinary, but highlights one of the most bizarre aspects of the whole business. For all Blair's touchy-feely posturing, his tearful tributes to popular celebrities, his 'cleansing' missions to Mexico and his government's obsession with comforting the population through their every tribulation, he is in fact one of the most gung-ho British prime ministers of modern times, who leaps at every opportunity provided by international crises to mobilise the armed forces and go to war.

If the Nanny State really has any faith in the benefits of 'counselling', the 'opening up' of 'emotional problems' and the pacifying effects of 'mainstreaming gender', it would presumably never need to go to war. All that Bush and Blair would have to do to end their differences with Osama bin Laden would be to install a large speaker system around his cave complex at Tora Bora and play

'All You Need Is Love' on a loop until he agrees to come out and go into counselling where he could openly discuss his 'issues' with a member of Social Services.

The constant attempts of the Nanny State to bracket every individual as a hapless victim of circumstance who needs his hand held as he faces each of life's difficulties do not even work domestically. Therefore, they cannot be expected to work in countries with cultures so vastly different to our own. It is symptomatic of the government's arrogance, however, to treat Afghan or Iraqi citizens as if they are merely unenlightened English people. This imperialistic attitude would seem to contradict much of what the Labour Party originally stood for, as it was founded by people who objected to the British Empire on moral grounds, because it both diverted state attention from domestic problems and treated foreigners as subjects of a monarch many of them had never heard of. Of particular concern to these idealists was the way that Britain rode roughshod over alien cultures, as if they had little or no independent validity. There seemed to be a general imperial belief that inside every Indian or Afghan was an Englishman struggling to get out.

New Labour seems to have rebranded itself so completely, however, that it behaves in exactly this patronising manner itself these days. The most surprising thing about this volte face is that we no longer actually have an empire. Undeterred, teams of misguided philanthropists are being paid by the government to impose Western therapeutic ideas on people who don't know who they are, don't know what they're talking about and don't know what they're doing in their country.

One of the particularly incompetent aspects of Western precision bombing has always been how imprecise it is. If the grieving parents of children bombed in Iraqi schools were approached by a friendly British counsellor, they might be forgiven for not seizing the chance to 'open up' and 'verbalise their pain'. Indeed, their reaction can better be imagined by picturing a similar scene in England. How would the family of a British soldier respond if a militant Iraqi Islamist knocked on their door and attempted to convert them? It is easier to imagine such a visitor being killed than being invited in for a cup of tea and a spiritual chat. Such a scenario only seems ludicrous because it isn't happening here. For the long-suffering inhabitants of cities like Kandahar or Basra, it is just one more indignity to which they are arrogantly subjected.

Back at home, the Nanny State's continuing insistence that our problems are not our own and that sharing them with a stranger will help us come to terms with them, inevitably leads to our wondering, that if we are not to blame for our problems and the various misfortunes that befall us, then who is? The inevitable result is that, instead of taking any personal responsibility for our lives, we increasingly pin the blame for the smallest mishap on someone else and, where possible, are encouraged to take everybody around us to court every time we trip over or feel unhappy.

Indeed, so hampered is every aspect of British life becoming by the constant fear of litigation, that the 'Compensation Culture' was condemned, in July 2004, by the Master of the Rolls, Lord Phillips, as eroding the very essence of British life. Lord Phillips particularly urged councils to stand up to the persistent attempts of parasitic lawyers and bring a halt to the outlawing of everything from children's swings to hanging baskets.

'I feel very strongly that individuals should not be restrained from carrying on sporting activities that involve risk, like hang-gliding and swimming,' Lord Phillips said in a newspaper interview. He then described a visit to a school in East Anglia, where he saw a sign by the swimming pool banning swimming alone.

> I said, 'I see the kids aren't allowed to swim without adult supervision.' 'Oh no,' they said, 'this is for the staff. Our insurers have said we can't let members of staff swim unsupervised.'

He then spoke of the case in 2003 where Law Lords condemned the 'Compensation Culture' when they ruled on a case brought by a man who broke his neck by diving into a flooded gravel pit. The five judges rejected the claim brought by John Tomlinson, stressing that the local council had put up clear 'no swimming' signs. In their judgment, they also warned of the 'evil consequences' of the compensation culture on liberty. Lord Phillips said he hoped that the ruling would be a warning to people who sued even when they knew they were taking a risk. It was, he said, 'a reaction to this type of nanny state approach'.

The worst thing about this phenomenon is how self-perpetuating it becomes. Once the Health and Safety fanatics encourage the idea that most of the horrific dangers that face us can be avoided through legislation, people tend to view the smallest accident as something that necessarily should have been avoided and that, therefore, someone else must be to blame. The litigation that follows only encourages more Health and Safety legislation, in a bid to prevent a repeat of the lawsuits.

Lord Phillips' intervention followed a flurry of reports in the press about how even the most innocent pursuits were being banned by councils in a bid to avoid expensive legal action. In one case, a children's swing hanging from a chestnut tree in the Hampshire village of Sleet was removed because the council feared it would be sued if there was an accident, even though generations of youngsters had played on the swing without recourse to a lawyer.

Colin Ettinger is president of the Association of Personal Injury Lawyers, and represents the interests of five thousand claimants' lawyers. His defence of the so-called 'compensation culture' is that '...if people can prove someone else was at fault, they are entitled to recover compensation'. He added, 'People should be brought to account if they have behaved in an unlawful way.' His comments skated over the fact that large numbers of people are being 'brought to account' whether they have acted 'unlawfully' or not. He fiercely denied the idea that people are more likely to claim damages now than ever before as well, declaring himself 'fed up to the back teeth with hearing about the so-called compensation culture'. He urged claimants to act responsibly, but presumably not so responsibly that the five thousand claimants' lawyers he represents have no work.

The government seems to support the idea of 'socially responsible' claims, perhaps because ministers are automatically well-disposed towards anybody urging greater 'responsibility' about anything. Tessa Jowell told *The Observer*:

> It's absolutely clear that schools are being deterred from

taking children on trips, either away in this country or abroad, because they fear the consequences of compensation if there's an accident. Everybody accepts it is valuable when children are growing up to have these experiences, but they need to be offered by people who are properly qualified.

As always Jowell's position was unclear. On the one hand she bemoaned the fact that schools are deterred from trips by fear of litigation but, on the other, she stressed the need for those in charge to be 'properly qualified'. In reality, this meant that teachers required extensive and costly training before they could be trusted to supervise children in the same way that teachers always have done.

The pressure for such superfluous 'qualifications' is a consequence of what the teaching unions term 'ambulance-chasing lawyers', who have targeted homes near schools, touting for business from dissatisfied parents. Chris Keates, a heavyweight in the teachers' union, summarised what is happening:

> There are leaflets being pushed through doors saying, 'Has your child had an accident at school? We can help!' We are talking about things that in the past would have been regarded as accidents – a child running across the playground and stumbling and cutting their knee. That has not in the past generated a solicitor's letter.

A spokesman for Education Secretary Charles Clarke, commented:

> ...it's through things like sport and school visits and that

> sort of enrichment that excitement about learning can be
> created. The culture that you can easily get sued – and it's
> not worth taking these kids out because if anything goes
> wrong you are going to get the blame for it – is a blockage
> in what we want to try and achieve.

The word 'blockage' is something of an understatement, given that the school system – still massively underfunded despite New Labour's motto of 'Education, education, education' at the 2001 election – is currently spending over £200 million a year fighting largely unnecessary lawsuits. Even Stephen Byers, a man not noted for averting a looming crisis, has warned:

> We are drifting pretty quickly into the American system,
> and we need to think carefully about whether we want to go
> down that road. You now have school play areas being
> closed down because of the risk of suing over play
> equipment.

Hearing the complaints of ministers such as Byers and Jowell, one might assume that the government intend to do something about it. Unfortunately, the Home Office recently blocked a bid by a cross-party group of MPs to change the law by drastically limiting the right to sue. Liberal Democrat MP Lembit Opek tabled a private member's bill with support from New Labour's own Frank Dobson which would have forced parents to sign legal 'certificates of risk' for children taking part in trips and activities, waiving rights to sue unless there is clear evidence of negligence. Another MP, Julian Brazier, spoke of the urgent need to reform, pointing out that even well-organised activities are being 'squeezed out' of children's lives. He said that '...it means that less adventurous children will become obese, and the more adventurous children will find ways of their own to do things which won't be at all safe'.

No parent will want to surrender their right to sue, however, particularly in such a litigation-friendly climate, and the bill seems doomed to failure. Meanwhile, the teachers' union has warned members not to lead out-of-school activities because of the litigation risk. As the pockets of the ambulance-chasing small claims experts, lawyers, and teacher training departments are all healthily lined by the above, it is, as always, the children who suffer, and are left bewildered by the latest cancellation in their school trip or the dismantling of more fun rides in the school's playground.

The government's talk of 'responsibility' neatly sidelines the fact that ultimate responsibility for the glut of compensation litigation rests with them. In 2000, New Labour decided to replace legal aid for claimants in personal injury suits with private lawyers operating on a no-win, no-fee arrangement. This was in addition to the existing iniquity that successful claimants still have to pay their own costs if the losing defendant has legal aid. The move was clearly designed as a money-saving exercise, and its consequences were equally clearly not thought through. The legislation removed any restriction on the amount claimants' lawyers can charge unsuccessful defendants (the 'success fee'), which is often very steep in order to compensate lawyers for the cases they might lose. The knock-on effects have included a massive upsurge in advertising, although Colin Ettinger cannot understand why people in his line of work are so reviled. 'We are portrayed as money-grabbing ambulance-chasers,' he moaned. He avoided mention, however, of the activities of some claims companies – the so-called 'claims farmers' who advertise for accident victims and then sell their names on to law firms.

The sharp increase in employers' liability premiums has been a defensive measure from companies terrified of being sued, and one which the insurance industry has explained simply as an inevitable result of living in a 'compensation culture'. The problem is that claims with no merit, which waste everybody's time, including the courts', are appearing with greater regularity than ever before, and the government is doing nothing to stop them. Arguably, it is doing less than nothing, because its attitude towards compensation litigation is so hypocritical. Having introduced the reforms which created the boom in the first place, it then attempted to 'talk tough' by condemning irresponsible claimants and talking, in Stephen Byers' words, of the need to avoid '...an American-style litigation goldrush'. When it is called upon to do anything practical, however, it has hidden behind the findings of an investigation by the non-independent Department for Work and Pensions, which neatly blamed the enormous rise in premiums on 'investment failures'. Beyond the fact that this is simply not an adequate explanation, it fails to acknowledge that some recent investments have failed precisely because new businesses cannot cope with oversized liability premiums. Meanwhile, the hallmark Blair's Britain is the sort of legal requirement that require food producers to label packets of nuts: 'Contains nuts.'

'Nuts' is a pretty good description of New Labour's attitude towards our wellbeing. Physical fitness is a particular bugbear for the government, which is convinced that the reponsibility for our weight and general health lies with them. Not that the Prime Minister can be expected to admit it. 'Being Prime Minister I should keep within the bounds of government policy,' he told BBC One's Breakfast with Frost in 2004. One almost expected him to follow up with 'but I'm not going to'. What he actually said was a little more devious, but amounted to pretty much the same thing:

> I do think we can get this issue in the wrong place. The prime responsibility for people looking after themselves is with people. I can't make people slimmer. What I can do is encourage, for example, sport in schools. We can give information, we can try to get the food industry to behave responsibly. But it is quite important we don't end up thinking the government can somehow determine whether people are large or small.

This little speech is a good paradigm of the Blair approach. He starts by stating his intention to keep within the bounds of government policy, but doesn't state what that policy is. Instead, he manoeuvres sideways by saying that it is all too easy to 'get this issue in the wrong place'. He then invites viewers to identify with his no-nonsense straight-talking approach by saying that he can't make people slimmer. This is followed by three ways in which he thinks he can make people slimmer. As a final flourish, he restates his initial position, presumably under the assumption that if people hadn't noticed his first falsehood, they wouldn't notice him contradicting it with a second.

This ingenious speech has a characteristic semblance of unity and consistency until you actually analyse it, at which point it reveals itself to be a worthless mixture of contradictory statements and oily disingenuousness. It also proves that, amongst all his other shortcomings, the Prime Minister isn't even a very good rhetorician. It is worth following his line of argument, however, simply to reveal quite how hollow he really is.

When ministers, particularly a Prime Minister, refer to what their administration 'can't' do, they are usually displaying the kind of odious false modesty which they consider most likely to make their 'surprise' achievements all the more impressive. Thus, when Blair claimed that 'I can't make people slimmer' what he actually meant was 'I can make people slimmer'.

Doctors polled by the British Medical Association were not so sure. Seventy-three per cent of those polled were convinced that the government would fail yet again to assign sufficient resources to make a real difference to public health. The findings, which were published in March, 2004, were accompanied by several doctors' comments, of which Nottingham consultant cardiothoracic surgeon David Beggs's were typical. He said that:

> ...it would be nice to think that sufficient funds would be given to public health to make a difference and to the acute sector to maintain and improve services. Sadly, I suspect the former will be a covert way of starving the acute sector and, in any event, the commercial pressures that encourage excess smoking, drinking and eating will win the day.

Had Dr Beggs not watched Breakfast with Frost? Had Blair not assured viewers that he would try to 'get the food industry to behave responsibly'? A government claiming to be 'Tough on crime, tough on the causes of crime' should have little difficulty bringing the (largely) crime-free food industry to heel, one might think. Petty criminals, though, do not make multi-million pound donations to the government, and nor do they agree to sponsor government schemes in return for a tacit slackening of regulations. The freedom that big food businesses have been given by New Labour to run riot is perhaps the single biggest reason why Britons are so fat. For Blair to admit as much, however, would be to bite the hand that feeds his party. That is why we get weak promises to 'try to get the food industry to behave responsibly' rather than more strident (but equally toothless) vows to bring the moral might of New Labour to bear on these corpulant fat cats. It is this which has led doctors like London consultant psychiatrist Warwick Onyeama into commenting:

> I have no confidence in any of the government's various statements about health improvement. The statements are simple 'media dazzlers' without any serious commitment to the systemic changes necessary to bring about real improvements in healthcare delivery.

Blair's first suggestion to get Britain slimmer was to '...encourage sport in schools'. Schools are a crucial battleground in the war on ill-health, for obvious reasons. The idea of making school food healthier has the support of Sustain, a group that campaigns for better food and wants to pressurize the Health Secretary to ensure that healthy eating programmes, including cookery lessons, are catered for in the national curriculum. Charlie Powell, the project officer at Sustain, explained in May 2004 that

> ...under our bill, junk foods won't be allowed to be sold in schools. It would be crazy to tell children to be healthy and then sell them junk food. The Food Standards Agency research shows that children often adopt the healthy option if given that option. We also need to make sure that school dinners reach a minimum nutritional value in schools. The Department for Education guidance on this is pitiful. Everyone would agree there is a crisis in children's health. We have to take it seriously. If we can't protect them in schools, where else can we? If we don't look after their health we're not being a responsible society. In secondary schools at the moment most food is covered in food technology. We hear about tasks being set for children to make a pizza box rather than create a healthy meal.

Powell's indignant complaints would seem to have full government support, not least because he has pushed all the right buttons about 'not being a responsible society' if children's school food is not nutritious enough. He was particularly sure that it would be 'crazy' to tell children to be healthy and then let them buy junk food. However you look at it, this meant that Sustain thought it was 'crazy' to give children any choice. Eric Spear, a former president of the National Association of Head Teachers, was sceptical about Sustain's demand to increase awareness of nutrition in schools, pointing out that

> Most heads do this already but the last thing we need is yet
> more legislation on what should be on the already
> overloaded curriculum. And really it's the parents we need
> to get to as much as the children. This generation of parents
> was brought up on junk food too.

A Department for Education and Skills spokeswoman said the
health of children was of 'paramount importance' and that therefore:

> School meals must meet minimum nutritional standards set
> to allow children to choose healthy and enjoyable school
> meals. Our healthy eating blueprint will provide them with
> full support and advice that they can access easily to
> promote healthy eating in schools. At school, giving a child
> a good diet can have a positive impact on all aspects of their
> education. They have more energy, they find it easier to
> concentrate, and it can help boost standards.

All this seems rather complicated. Sustain think it is 'crazy' to let
children choose what they eat, the government that supports it
declares that it is of 'paramount importance' that children are
'allowed to choose' what they eat, and the children themselves are, as
usual, left thoroughly bewildered, and hungry. Not for New Labour
the idea of a state school serving basically nutritious food which
pupils have to eat. Children, not knowing whether they are part of a
'crazy' system or one of 'paramount importance', must consult a
government-sponsored 'healthy eating blueprint' before entering the

school canteen. It may be designed in the bests interests of the child, but New Labour have made school dinnertime a more complicated part of a child's life than a physics test. And what of Tony Blair's simple promise to 'encourage sport in schools'? Here we may have the answer to all the confusion.

Everybody knows that junk food is bad for you. Everybody, that is, except the schoolchildren unlucky enough to attend schools like the one in Birmingham managed by Cadbury Schweppes. George Monbiot exposed the kind of 'education' these children were getting in *Captive State* in 2000. What would Tony Blair make of an education pack that explained to children: 'Chocolate is a wholesome food that tastes really good. It is fun to eat at any time of the day and gives you energy and important nutrients that your body needs to work properly'? Or of the primary schools in Dudley, Teesside and North Somerset managed by McDonald's, where children are asked to find names of the company's products in a 'word puzzle'. Or to choose matching images of its french fries and milkshakes? Or to learn the words to that charming nursery folksong 'Old McDonald had a Store'? Perhaps he actually approves of them, given that he invented the scheme in 1998 that handed the management of struggling schools over to private businesses.

The procedure was euphemised as a 'partnership between businesses, parents and schools'. Except that the schools had no choice and the parents weren't consulted. Education Action Zones (or EAZs) were described as 'the test bed for the education system of the twenty-first century', whereby ailing schools could be taken over by businesses which would then, effectively, run them. Simultaneous with their inception was the arrival for the first time in British schools of marketing billboards, well aware of the truth of McDonald's *Operations Manual* assertion, 'Schools offer excellent opportunities. Not only are they a high traffic [sales] generator, but students are some of the best customers you could have.' Eric Spear fumed that:

> I'm entirely opposed...but a lot of schools need the sponsorship from fizzy drinks and chocolatey things and crisps. It's an outrageous situation that we have to rely on that sort of sponsorship.

Outrageous indeed, but manfully countered by Tony Blair's promise to 'encourage sport in schools'. Sadly, this particular Nanny's exhortation to run outside and play for a while came in partnership with Cadbury's *Get Active!* scheme, whereby children were encouraged to buy chocolate bars in return for school sports equipment.

Arrangements like *Get Active!* are commonplace. Walkers' Crisps are almost solely responsible for the upkeep of school libraries, for example, but the real problem with *Get Active!* was that a scheme which aimed to make children thin was directly dependent on making them fat at the same time. Sports Minister Richard Caborn supported the scheme, but the leader of the Commons, Peter Hain, described the endorsement as 'pretty indefensible'. Tessa Jowell responded that the scheme was 'entirely defensible', pointing out that '...it's not so much that children are getting fat because they are eating significantly more, they're getting fatter because they're taking much less exercise'. Jowell's observation was unsupported by all the available evidence, which blames diet almost exclusively for the rise in obesity.

Also, the fact that *Get Active! would* result in children eating 'significantly more' appeared not to occur to her. Transport Minister Kim Howells leaped to Caborn's defence as well, claiming that '...I know Richard Caborn and he is a great minister.' Thank god for that. Furthermore, Howells elaborated, '...he works ceaselessly to try to encourage people to take more exercise.'

The absurdity of encouraging children to gorge themselves on Cadbury's bars in order to pay for equipment the government should be buying in the first place somewhat overshadowed the almost equal ridiculousness of a cabinet minister whose job was to 'work ceaselessly to try to encourage people to take more exercise'. Howells was not done yet, either. 'A chocolate bar once a week is not going to wreak havoc on anybody's health, especially if they are taking more exercise,' he sneered. Such a modest rate of consumption could well wreak havoc at school games time, however, given that five thousand four hundred and forty chocolate wrappers were required for a single goal net. At one chocolate bar a week, that would take a school one hundred and four years to earn on the Get Active! exchange rate.

Furthermore, even by the most ferocious capitalist standards, Cadbury's had struck a fantastically good deal with the government. At an average cost of thirty-five pence, 5440 chocolate bars are worth £1904. A standard school goal net costs about £15. As Howells concluded, 'We have got to be sensible about these things.' Meanwhile, a spokeswoman for Cadbury's said that '...the scheme was last year and it's now reached the end of its natural lifespan. We're in the process of redeeming the tokens.'

Whilst schoolchildren constantly scurried off into the trees to collect footballs pounded time after time into netless goalmouths and the government attempted to defend the indefensible, Cadbury's enjoyed the kind of profit it had only dreamed of under Thatcher. The spokeswoman for the confectionery company said a lot more than she knew when she concluded that '...there's nothing really for us to say'.

Blair's other health pledge was to assure viewers of *Breakfast with Frost* that the government could be trusted to 'give information'. An example of the kind of information the government gives was displayed at the end of May, 2004, when the report on the obesity crisis 'sweeping the nation' focused on the death of an overweight three-year-old girl described in Chapter Three, which '...offered a powerful insight into the crisis posed to the nation's health'. The child had been suffering from an over-pressurised windpipe, making it difficult for her to breathe.

The condition is known as sleep apnoea, and was reported by Sheila McKenzie, a specialist in children's breathing problems. She was reportedly 'horrified' by the use of her patient's case as a case study of the fatal consequences of child obesity, not least because the girl had died of a rare hereditary genetic condition unrelated to her diet. It was much easier for the government to achieve 'awareness' by saying she had died because she was too fat, however. It mattered hardly at all that Mackenzie immediately told other paediatricians that she had been misquoted and misreported, because the tabloids now had their headlines. A tedious government health report become a front-page sensation thanks to banners like *The Sun*'s 'Fat and Dead...at three!'

The doctor at Cambridge University's department of clinical

biochemistry who diagnosed the girl's condition said:

> I was appalled and I must say I felt for the parents and
> family of this child. The clear implication was that the child
> had been overfed, with bad parents, resulting in severe
> obesity and her death. That is simply not true.

As a rebuttal of a government health report, you can't get much worse than a world expert describing the findings as 'simply not true'. MP Richard Taylor was happy to defend the poor girl's scapegoating, however, by explaining that '...as it is children we have to get at more than anybody else, it was felt that this was a way of emphasising the danger for children'. Even when the information being given was 'simply not true'! Steve O'Rahilly, the head of the Cambridge department where the girl was diagnosed, stated that:

> We need to inject a degree of honesty into this debate and
> be a little more humble in the face of the real uncertainties
> about the causes of obesity. Ignoring the role of inherited
> factors in determining people's susceptibility to becoming
> fat is not only bad science, it also helps to perpetuate the
> blame culture which tends to permeate this field. If we
> applied more science and less political positioning we
> might get some clearer ideas for solutions.

Until O'Rahilly's words are heeded, however, we are left with a government whose idea of 'giving information' is to misrepresent things so completely that they are 'simply not true'.

Blair's third vow was to 'try to get the food industry to behave responsibly', and it is perhaps here most of all that his insincerity, and the insincerity of the government as a whole, is exposed. Never before has a government relied so heavily on big business handouts, even if they do result in Ronald McDonald running our schools, and the pledge to 'try to get the food industry to behave responsibly' must be understood in this context. Perhaps Blair's obsessive need to nanny the nation has arisen from a guilty conscience. The government persistently tells us we are unhealthy and ought to go to the gym an unrealistic number of times a day but, in their heart of hearts, they know that their policies have made healthy, responsible living harder than ever before.

The food industry is currently lobbying Westminster as never before as well, and a leaked memo in May 2004 revealed what kind of nonsense is being bandied about in the corridors of power. Essentially, advertisers and manufacturers have exploited their direct access to the heart of government to fiercely safeguard their sales revenue and commercial standing. Put simply, they have fought action on health at every turn to protect their products' reputation. MP Debra Shipley has long campaigned for tighter controls on marketing for children, and she observed that:

> The lobbying is now intense. On the one side are all the health organisations you can think of, and on the other the vested interests in the industry. If the government takes no action, we know the vested interests won't.

It is already too late. A joint letter signed by such bigwigs as Niall FitzGerald, president of the Advertising Association which spent

£452m in 2002, and John Sunderland, chairman of New Labour favourite Cadbury Schweppes, has suggested that the government should focus on a 'joint public health campaign' and promote 'ten tips for better health' rather than enforce statutory labelling of food detrimental to health. The campaign should 'stress the importance of individual responsibility' and advise people to 'try to drink more fluids'. Presumably manufactured by Schweppes. It is a clear case of big businesses dictating policy to government, and telling them to keep nannying rather than to take any action. A letter sent to Richard Caborn (personally endorsed by colleagues as a 'great minister') from Cadbury Schweppes actually complained that 'the food industry is being viewed as part of the problem'. Rather than treating such letters with the contempt they deserve, the government is complicit in the process of letting the industry off the hook, not least by receiving advance copy of food PR for approval. 'Dear Richard', wrote the minister's old friend Cadbury Schweppes in May 2004:

> We are enclosing some of the key messages which we will
> be trying to get across in the weeks to follow. We do hope
> that you can endorse these as a sensible way forward...

New Labour does not have the strength to stand up to the industries which fund it, so it blames the public for its own misdemeanours.

Everything in our Nanny State is explained by 'personal responsibility' but the only one refusing to share in that responsibility is Nanny herself.

6 Sentence first, verdict afterwards

'Let the jury consider their verdict,' the King said, for about the twentieth time that day.
'No, no!' said the Queen. 'Sentence first – verdict afterwards.'
'Stuff and nonsense!' said Alice loudly. 'The idea of having the sentence first!'

Lewis Carroll, *Alice's Adventures in Wonderland*

Alice's indignation in the Wonderland courts of justice is hardly surprising. To give a sentence before knowing the verdict negates the entire point of a trial. Indeed, it turns the whole concept of justice on its head. It is the kind of thing that only happens in fantasy or in nonsense stories by people like Lewis Carroll. It is certainly not something George Orwell mentioned in his work of grim prophecy, *1984*. The Orwellian vision of the future was nightmarishly totalitarian, 'a boot stamping on a human face – forever', but it wasn't totally absurd. Visions of the future do not tend to encompass the inconceivable. Forward-thinking political philosophers like John Locke or Jean-Jacques Rousseau could, therefore, never have predicted New Labour. Truly to get a glimpse of a future in Blair's Britain we must turn, of course, to *Alice's Adventures in Wonderland.* Unfortunately, however, there is one crucial difference. Alice can tell the court 'You're nothing but a pack of cards!' and see the whole edifice come tumbling down before she wakes up saying 'Oh, I've had such a curious dream!'

Although watching the government muddle its way through ever more draconian and unnecessary legislation does at times feel similarly surreal, it is more of a nightmare than a dream, and one that warrants a stronger description than merely 'curious'; and the desire to see the Nanny State collapse like so many playing cards intensifies with every restrictive new policy that is introduced. Not only is the government apparently involved in a bid to break every possible record for the number of previously harmless activities it is possible to criminalise, but it is also arming itself with an increasingly illiberal arsenal of legal powers with which to wage war on this new raft of 'criminals'.

One of the proposed new measures to combat the 'new' threat of terrorism, for example, is that the standard of evidence required to convict in certain cases should be lowered from 'beyond reasonable doubt' to 'on the balance of probabilities'. Blair countered criticism of this reactionary suggestion with the proviso that the change would only apply to the very worst of crimes. This effectively suggested that the weight of evidence required to secure a conviction should be inversely related to the gravity of the crime for which a suspect is being tried. The treatment of the detainees in Guantanamo Bay is a frightening example of this. Our government is currently allowing its own citizens to be held indefinitely by another nation in a prison camp. The lack of declared evidence against them is cited by both Blair and Bush as proof of their criminal cunning and of the immense danger they pose to our societies. To less crazed minds, the lack of declared evidence against them makes their incarceration look totally unjust. The government argues that if they are ruthless terrorists, they must not be allowed the freedom to terrorise us. Its only response to the reasonable question 'But what if they aren't?' is to say 'They are.'

Since they are not prepared to back up such certainty with the alleged evidence, we just have to trust them. Unfortunately, it is harder to trust Blair's government than any other government in memory because it lies and spins the whole time. Thus we see the vital tenet of Habeas Corpus violated, but can do nothing about it except conduct a playground argument with the school bully.

Guantanamo could be seen as the result of the government being pushed into a position where it has to act in such an extreme manner because of public perceptions of the severity of the current terrorist threat. It is extremely misleading to peddle the notion that terrorism presents an unprecedented threat to this country, however. Its instigators may now be in Tora Bora rather than Belfast, but the fear of a surprise attack on Britain by terrorists is one we have lived with since at least 1969. The IRA have, to date, done far more damage to the country than al-Qaeda and its affiliates, and yet we are constantly told by the government that the fear of a terror attack is a completely new problem. This is not to suggest that we shouldn't worry about it, shrugging our shoulders as if to say 'we've had worse', but nor should we allow the government to force through new legislation undemocratically. The justification that desperate times call for desperate measures is simply not good enough in a country which has been terrorised for over thirty years by its own neighbour. However, such extraordinarily unjust measures are not just confined to those suspected of planning a devastating 'jihad' against the country. Similar measures have been mooted to combat the potential behaviour of naughty children.

Again, this affront to a civilised system of justice is one that Orwell, with the considerable resource of his paranoid imagination, failed to predict. Such gross inversions of justice are set to become the norm, however, particularly if bodies such as the Youth Inclusion and Support Panel (or YISP) have their way. This particular government-sponsored initiative aims to target children yet to commit an offence in order to reduce their likelihood of offending. Beyond the suspicion that David Blunkett has exhausted the imaginations of both Carroll and Orwell and started to steal his ideas from Steven Spielberg, whose *Minority Report* is about just such a hellish future society, there is the obvious concern that children singled out as 'likely' troublemakers will feel obliged to live up to their elders' expectations.

Bob Ashford, Head of Prevention for the Youth Justice Board, is unconcerned by such objections. 'The scheme is not rocket science, nor is it ethically questionable,' he somewhat nonsensically declares. He views the YISP as a crucial tool of social rectification, lamenting the fact that '...in the past, local agencies have worked in such a fragmented way that children who have not yet committed a crime have slipped through the net'.

Given that the overwhelming majority of children have 'not yet committed a crime', the only logical conclusion to Ashford's scheme would be to incarcerate every child in Britain. This leaves him unmoved because 'it has been proved beyond any doubt that if children slip into crime, there is an appallingly high likelihood of them going on to become persistent or violent adult offenders.' As the Youth Justice Board evidently considers 'if' and 'whether or not' interchangeable, their scheme is questionable in the extreme. In Ashford's peculiarly punitive Utopia, it is a matter for grave concern that children who have not done anything wrong are not being punished. It is as if the Red Queen of Wonderland has the ear of the government.

The government itself, movingly epitomised by married father-of-four Tony Blair, understands with Ashford that 'the life chances of children are hugely influenced by their earliest experiences, which is why access to post-natal support, parenting classes and early years provision are so important for a fair society'. A child could be scarred for life by witnessing the distress caused to its mother by the unavailability of 'parenting classes', but being victimised itself for crimes it hasn't committed will seemingly not adversely affect its 'life-chances', and is consistent with the concept of a 'fair society'. Ashford has so far been granted seventy thousand pounds to pursue this extraordinary experiment, but as soon as research is done into the inevitable success of his program, that figure will rise exponentially. No research was deemed necessary before authorising the scheme. Sharon Moore of the Children's Society is, unsurprisingly, wholly against the idea. Her understated summation is simply that 'I fear the results'. She might as well be referring to New Labour's cavalier reformation of British justice in general.

Britain's descent into such crime-ridden paranoia that our government funds schemes to apprehend innocent children has escalated recently. This is partly because New Labour are disproportionately obsessed with the extent of the problem. Before the Second World War there was comparatively little violence in society, but the number of indictable criminal offences reached a peak in 1951, doubling the number found as recently as 1938.

The police escaped censure despite the rise, and the respect they commanded in society was still large enough for the notorious 'Let him have it!' murder of a policeman by Derek Bentley (although his underage accomplice Christopher Craig actually pulled the trigger) in 1952 to cause public outrage. The execution of the mentally subnormal Bentley, already in handcuffs at the time of the shooting, caused no similar wave of protest.

Those concerned with social improvement were more interested in prison conditions, particularly those in the Borstals for Young Offenders, and probation. Despite the Thatcherite insistence on treating them separately, crime rose throughout the second half of the century in keeping with unemployment. The number of recorded offences in 1981 was three million, but a decade of bitter social strife saw that figure almost double, and by 1996 the police were claiming that less than half the crimes committed in the country were being reported. Households in tower blocks and housing estates were the greatest victims, but the sensationalised accounts of isolated atrocities like the murder of James Bulger in 1993 contributed to a sense of unprecedented moral depredation in society at large, which both major parties blamed on their inheritance from a previous government. Outside Whitehall, the situation appeared equally grim, with such 'ordinary' criminals such as Charlie Kray lamenting that '...even the most hardened criminal a few years ago would have helped an old lady across the road and given her a few quid if she was skint'. Thatcher's 'enterprise culture' appeared to have killed off such decency for good.

How to deal with the increase in crime, and its causes, has divided opinion and political parties, as well as the police. The hugely controversial Criminal Justice and Public Order Act of 1995 gave enormous power to the Home Office, whose powers had already been substantial before the new legislation. The Act appeared to confirm George Bernard Shaw's observation that 'anarchism is a game at which the police can beat you', given the new opportunities it afforded for misuse of authority. It included among its provisions restriction of the right to silence, increased police power to take action in suspicious circumstances and a tougher stance on trespassers and squatters. John Major responded to criticism with the extraordinary claim that '...society needs to condemn a little more and understand a little less.' The one arguable virtue of such a worrying sentiment, however, is that he was prepared to express it.

Tony Blair has picked up where Michael Howard left off when it comes to justice, but he has done so while saying that

> A modern civic society, underpinned by reformed public
> services and an active welfare state, won't emerge simply

through better laws, tougher enforcement of obligations, sanctions and more police. As well as modernising the Criminal Justice System and tackling anti-social behaviour we also need to revive the spirit of community and social cohesion. As Martin Luther King said, 'Laws restrain the heartless, they cannot change the heart.'

Once one has recovered not just from the shock of Tony Blair presuming to quote and implicitly share in King's moral dignity, but has also accepted that he is proposing to 'change our hearts' himself, it is worth considering how he intends to go about it.

Our Prime Minister clearly has the wisdom to see that it will take more than 'better laws, tougher enforcement of obligations, sanctions and more police' to achieve something Christ himself viewed as an eternal struggle. An analysis of New Labour's largely incoherent justice reforms does, however, eventually reveal a spectacularly mismanaged program which can be summed up as follows: 'better' laws, tougher enforcement of obligations, sanctions and more police. No legislation is yet in place specifically to 'change our hearts', but '...citizenship is now part of the national curriculum and the National Lottery will put an extra £750 million into new sports and communities facilities.'

In real terms, divorced from Blair's sickly idealism, New Labour are perpetually encroaching on our freedom and right to take responsibility for ourselves in the name of progress. For all the rubbish about changing our hearts, and the disingenuous distancing from a very similar Conservative position, New Labour are merely the latest government to confirm Plato in saying that '..."just" or "right" means nothing but what is in the interest of the stronger party.'

Since 1997, the 'stronger party' has been a Labour Government determined to improve our society by bringing the state into ever-closer contact with the individual. Civil society has historically been understood as an area not normally governed by the state, but New Labour is no normal government. As political commentator Andrew Rawnsley noted, in 2002, this government is what the Americans call a 'wheel-spinning' one. He wrote:

> Exceedingly busy, hyperactive, even a manic government'.
> In the last parliamentary session, 'ministers broke all records by passing into law more pages of legislation than in any previous session, but the government is so frantically creating new powers that ministers neglect to ask themselves whether those powers are useable by those to whom they are given.

In other words, the legislation may well be a complete waste of time and money. Furthermore, the powers the government is giving itself are inevitably being created by taking power away from others. We still prize our liberty above all else, but are so keen to safeguard it that we fail to appreciate that a government with a massive majority is a disaster for democracy. Gerald Ford wryly observed that 'If the government is big enough to give you everything you want, it is big enough to take away everything you have...' and New Labour's reformatory zeal is Ford's observation incarnate.

Blair tends to pitch his personal vision of the big state through his repeated insistence that we are united as a community through our shared understanding and respect for one another.

> Respect is what makes us a community, not merely a group of isolated individuals. It makes real a new contract between citizen and state.

This cloying statement is nearly free from meaning, other than that there genuinely is a 'new contract' between citizen and state, whereby the state removes our power. Complacency and apathy tend to mask the truth that power should reside with the people in a democracy, and any government gifting itself unprecedented powers of interference is behaving undemocratically. New Labour's legislative zeal has almost entirely been directed at centralising a huge number of powers. Given that Britain is a democracy, this cannot but mean that their gain is our loss.

What makes Tony Blair such a dangerous Prime Minister is that he sees no limit to his democratic remit. It would be irredeemably cynical to dismiss the possibility that society can improve, but it is equally naïve to think that a political party can create a society 'free from racism, prejudice and intolerance'. That Blair is prepared to state this as an achievable political aim is not just risible, it is actually irresponsible.

It isn't even politically advisable, because the inevitable failure of his Utopian vision will result in his premiership itself being seen as a failure, judged on its own terms. What is even worse is that he can dismiss the 1945 'big state' precisely because it '...wrongly believed it could solve every social problem' and claims that he sees the folly in an 'overbearing paternalistic state'. But once more, the Third Way between destructive individualism and an overbearing 'Daddy' state is a Nanny state. When he speaks of a society 'marked by vandalism, violent crime and the loss of civility' it is the third aspect of the problem that he sees as the cause of the others. The ambiguous notion of 'respect' is the one that Blair seems to care most about, and its absence for him 'evokes the sense that the moral fabric of community is unravelling.'

The average victim of crime, one suspects, would hardly be mollified if the criminal said 'please' and 'thank you', but for New Labour it is the key issue because '...it is petty crime and public nuisance that causes so much distress to people; vandalism, graffiti, low-level aggression and violence'. Even 'anti-social tenants and their anti-social landlords can make life hell for their community', and so New Labour '...will give local authorities new powers to license private-sector landlords, ensuring that landlords and their tenants behave responsibly'.

Increasing the amount of stress and pointless bureaucracy involved in renting a house by giving 'local authorities new powers' does not immediately seem like a solution to Britain's social ills. It is, however, one of the very few pieces of actual legislation to be gleaned from Blair's hopeless speeches. Even here there are difficulties – what precisely does 'responsible behaviour' consist of legally? Notwithstanding an avowed intention to 'overhaul the justice system', Blair constantly churns out highly subjective phrases which would give any British court nightmares if they had to give them legal application. It is a particularly irritating aspect of his leadership style because, as a barrister, he is better versed than most in the ways of the legal system. He must *know* that a lot of what he says is pure verbiage because he spent the early part of his professional life studying and then practising law himself. You can imagine the young Tony Blair pumping his fist in the air after another courtroom victory gained by deconstructing the finer points of civil law. He would have been as quick as anyone to pounce on a phrase as woolly as 'responsible behaviour' and question its worth in legal application. One of the ironies of his style of government is that, despite the mindboggling proliferation of new laws created by his administration, he is extremely reluctant to descend from the level of idealistic speechifying to explain himself.

He has become the kind of person his younger self would have ripped apart in court but, to carry the image further, whether the jury would have acquitted him is debatable.

The most damaging aspect of Blair's obsession with a 'tougher approach to anti-social behaviour' is that it is far from being one of Britain's most pressing problems. Neither is it the root cause of many other problems. It is extremely difficult, for example, to see any immediate link between incivility and the terrible decline in the NHS or state education. Naughty children may be a headache for doctors and teachers alike, but they cannot be blamed for a crippling shortage of funds. Blair would rather avoid the issue.

He began one pontification with the seemingly throwaway remark 'however much schools and hospitals improve...'. Slipped in as the preamble to another point, he must have hoped it would go unnoticed, but reprinted it must have made every parent and patient in the land cry 'Whaaaat?'

Fewer people than ever before are applying for teaching posts, because the last thing young people want to do is go back to an institution as decrepit as our educational system. New Labour has fiddled with the National Curriculum so irresponsibly that Shakespeare questions in GCSE exams have literally *nothing* to do with Shakespeare. A sample question in an exam supposedly about *Henry IV Part One* ran as follows : 'Prince Hal has a difficult relationship with his dad. Do you or any of your friends find it tough to relate to either of your parents?'. God alone knows how children were supposed to respond to the question if their answer was 'No'.

As for the improvement of hospitals, there have never been such long NHS waiting lists and bed shortages. The government regularly attempts to explain away this awkward fact by claiming that we are unhealthier than ever before, eating fatty foods, smoking too much and drinking excessively. Not only is such an explanation deeply offensive to the electorate it still (apparently) relies on for its support, it also isn't true. We are healthier than ever before, have greater access to health information, treat our bodies more carefully and live longer than previous generations. The NHS is in such a bad state because it is underfunded and incompetently run by people who have been trained to manage profit-making businesses, and maximise their potential toward that end only.

Blair reckons that '...if people walk out of their doors and are confronted by abuse, vandalism, anti-social behaviour, they will never feel secure or able to take advantage of new opportunities'. This is patently untrue to the point of offensiveness, and wilfully disregards the whole concept of triumphing over adversity. The social ills Blair obsesses over are intensely undesirable, but to believe that they can be cured by legislation is not simply misguided, it is actively irresponsible. Not only does such a belief divert attention from more constructive solutions, such as improved education, but it fosters the notion that nothing can be achieved in an imperfect society. In fact, it largely destroys the idea of achievement altogether, because, to paraphrase Oliver Cromwell, where is achievement in the absence of strife?

New Labour's commitment to tackling crime is so wide-ranging that coherent policy comes a poor second to pointless new legislation. Vandalism is such a terrible social evil, however, that new schemes to heal the scars it has created cannot wait. The fight against vandalism is so important, in fact, that it is necessary to disrupt children in their classrooms to pursue it. In May, 2004, police officers began entering classrooms to photograph and record the scribbles of pupils:

> Using the latest mobile phone technology to identify distinctive signatures and styles. Images of etchings are captured on camera phones, emailed to police headquarters and stored in a database of graffiti 'tags', the trademark sign of the urban street 'artist'. Detectives can then compare them with images of spray paint vandalism in towns and cities

If this new initiative were not extremely distracting to children attempting to concentrate on their lessons, it could be seen as merely a huge waste of public money. The fact that it could potentially create an atmosphere of persecution in an environment that ought to feel secure makes it more than a misuse of public funds. It is also perilously close to the Red Queen's 'Sentence first – verdict afterwards!' principle of justice, given that ordinary children will have their doodles photographed, logged and filed for use as evidence on the off chance that they are a dangerous vandal. What makes the scheme especially iniquitous, however, is not the havoc it will wreak in the nation's schools. It is the fact that it is doomed to failure. It would be almost impossible to convict a graffiti artist on the basis that a defacement of public property looked a bit like some scratchings in the back of a biology textbook. In many cases, such 'evidence' would not even be admissable.

Civil liberties groups have of course condemned the scheme outright, with a spokesman for Liberty stating that it is 'gimmicky'. Just how gimmicky will depend on which mobile phone giant the metropolitan police force does a sponsorship deal with. Talks are currently being held with Orange, but no doubt graffiti-detection technology will be developed across the board by all their competitors in a bid to snare the deal. Another civil liberties spokesman pointed out, 'It doesn't seem to get anywhere near the complex causes of graffiti.' She went to lampoon the idea of "experts" identifying a graffiti artist by his doodles to the court. She commented, 'I am sceptical that it would be foolproof.' In other words, this 'new, simpler, tougher approach to anti-social behaviour' is inefficient, ineffective, more complicated and, ultimately, softer on vandals who cannot be convicted on the basis of such ridiculous evidence. Such is the willingness of Blair's government to pour money into hopeless and often unpleasant new legal initiatives that it is far from being unique, however.

Blair's love of curfews is one particularly ridiculous new 'measure' to create 'respect'. The rush to impose curfews on city centres and housing estates has come, seemingly, from nowhere. It is a development of a policy that has been in place since Blair took office in 1997, giving police the power to order the under-tens to go home. Even the children concerned could see that the police would not be able to differentiate between a nine-year-old and a ten-year-old, however, and reassured themselves that officers' time would remain more profitably taken up in the pursuit of criminals than in monitoring toddlers' bedtimes. Even the police in Enid Blyton's Toytown are more concerned with the Naughty Monkey than with when Noddy turns his light out. Far from admitting the pointlessness of the legislation, Blair declared the curfew a great success and extended it to include an upper age limit of fifteen. To date, the Avon and Somerset, Bedfordshire, Cambridgeshire, Cleveland, Cumbria, Essex, Hampshire, Humberside, Metropolitan, North Wales, Nottingham, South Wales, Surrey, Sussex, Warwickshire and West Mercia police forces have received the power to apprehend children under the age of sixteen out of doors after nine o'clock and take them home, where they must stay until six the next morning, on pain of a hefty fine or imprisonment. Getting up early to do a paper round could land unlucky children in jail. That the children may be causing no trouble at the time of their apprehension is no defence.

The horror of child murder seems to bring out the worst in New Labour, who are determined not to accept responsibility for presiding over a society where such things happen. When ten-year-old

Damilola Taylor was murdered on a Peckham housing estate in 2000, Home Secretary Jack Straw gravely intoned that '...we need to create a responsible society where each of us takes responsibility, not only for our own actions, but also for the way society and our immediate community behaves'. David Blunkett went a little further, claiming, without any proof whatsoever, that passers-by had left Damilola for dead, and stating that '...we have got to create a society where people do not run away from anything, but face up to it'. Perhaps Blunkett enjoyed the Biblical 'Good Samaritan' overtones his embellishment gave the story or perhaps he thought that the invention of such details would obscure the hypocrisy of criticising those who 'run away' from problems rather than 'facing up' to them.

Damilola's own father certainly seemed to have Blunkett and colleagues rather than his son's killers in mind when he said that his son's death proved in Britain that 'family values have been bastardised and allowed to go to the dogs. Parents don't care about work any more and instead rely on social security to take care of their children.'

The sad truth is that senseless murder can never be 'explained', but it is only natural for a grieving parent to lash out at the social conditions in which his family live. Far less easy to condone is a government which blames 'society' for such crimes in response. New Labour's attitude towards blame and responsibility is spectacularly inconsistent. Tony Blair in particular is obsessed with concepts of 'civility' and 'individual responsibility', and yet his policies perpetually encroach on the individual's autonomy and corrode our sense of community. New Labour constantly promotes the idea that it is far better equipped to look after us than we are to look after ourselves, and yet every time such intrusive statism fails the government blames individuals for neglecting their 'responsibilities'. Sickeningly, the complex circumstances behind tragedies like Damilola Taylor's death are ignored by the government, who attempt to take political advantage of shocking incidents to force through new legislation.

Peckham is one of Europe's biggest regeneration zones, but 'regeneration' has only benefited private property developers, while the stock of decent council housing has diminished. In November, 2000, Deputy Prime Minister John Prescott hailed the Peckham Partnership Project as a '...shining example of what can be done to renew deprived neighbourhoods'. At a cost of £260 million, 4,000 apartment blocks were demolished and replaced with just 2,000 new homes. In protest, a major tenants' body passed a motion of no confidence in the project's management. Mike Rahman, development manager for the Peckham Partnership Tenants and Residents Forum complained that '...people still haven't got jobs and health has not improved'.

Even worse, about 750 of the 2,000 new homes were sold to private owners. Rahman commented that '...there is the belief that if you bring middle class people into the area their affluence will rub off on ordinary people. But they will not raise the standards of living for ordinary people.' David Page, housing consultant for the charity the Joseph Rowntree Foundation, issued a report after Damilola Taylor's murder called *Communities in the balance: The reality of social exclusion on housing estates*. It emphasised that there had been twenty years of under-investment in housing in the area and noted the connection between poverty, deprivation and crime. Jack Straw responded to the report with a level of sensitivity and sophistication unusual even for a New Labour minister when he flatly stated, '...it's not the buildings that killed Damilola Taylor, but some people.'

David Blunkett, presumably bereft of the earlier inspiration which had led him to invent details about the murder, decided to play it safe and respond to the Rowntree Foundation's report by talking about Chris Tarrant. He denounced the '"me first"' society, whose selfishness '...is typified by the hit television quiz show *Who Wants To Be A Millionaire?*' Damilola's parents no doubt nodded in agreement, relieved that the root causes of their son's horrific murder were being tackled head-on by ministers excoriating quiz shows rather than studying damning inner-city housing reports that made clear the link between urban deprivation and violent crime.

In a very short space of time, Damilola Taylor's death had been seamlessly transformed into a justification for the government's proposed introduction of child curfews, keeping children aged nine to fifteen indoors after ten p.m, with Straw telling the BBC:

> If you get kids racketing around when they're ten, eleven or twelve, out of order, not under proper control, not knowing where the boundaries are and also dealing with all conflicts through fights, when they're seventeen, eighteen and nineteen that's going to spill out to more violence on the streets.

Ken Livingstone, the newly elected London mayor who had

claimed he would redress the 'arc of poverty' in London, announced a £60 million plan to boost police numbers on the capital's street by 1,250, in the '...fight against the knife culture which killed Damilola.' Many teachers, social workers and others opposed to New Labour's repressive response to every social problem asked themselves, in the absence of concrete evidence that children were involved in the death of Damilola, what it said about the problems and crisis within society as a whole. No attempt was made to delve into such questions by the government. Instead, ineffective and frankly medieval 'curfews' were proposed to divert attention from a serious discussion of the appalling social conditions that had been created in many inner-city areas. Never has a government so confused cause and effect, or been so cynically prepared to exploit tragedy. One of the Nanny State's greatest skills is its adeptness at assuming authority without effectively exercising it. The unfortunate difference between New Labour and a real nanny is that a real nanny is answerable to the parents who employ her.

On the first anniversary of Damilola Taylor's death in November 2001, Blair had the temerity to site himself at the centre of attention at a Peckham memorial service attended by the entire Taylor family. But he was still talking of how different the future would be, rather than about what he had done in the last year. 'In many ways what he represented is something that will have a lasting legacy,' Blair told mourners. Many present must also have suspected that the dead child represented short-term political capital. 'The best tribute is in trying to help in the remaking of his local community,' the Prime Minister explained, knowing full well that council housing in Peckham had been halved in the face of a vote of no confidence in the development by residents. Blair also trotted out the dangerous assumption that those who killed Damilola would not have thought to do so in an area with better facilities.

Alan Kabia, coordinator of the Peckham Positive Project advice centre set up at the top of the stairwell where Damilola was found, said that nothing was different:

> The people who did this are all still around in Peckham. Who knows if it could happen again – nothing has changed since Damilola has died. Politicians come from all corners but it's still the same. The problems have not gone away just because some troublemakers have gone. People are still afraid, especially people who do night shifts. They will leave for work really early and then hang about at work until it is light so they can come home

He added there were still dozens of families living in condemned buildings, as well as an unknown number of squatters. David Richards of the SB tenants' office said, 'The new buildings go up but the point is who you move into them. Maybe the wrong people will get moved in, and then you're in a murder zone again.' In fact, the area around the notorious North Peckham Estate where Damilola died was left unchanged until it was announced that Blair himself would be visiting, at which point the drug dealers were temporarily moved on and the shrubs outside the youth centre were spruced up. The message in Peckham seems to be that a government only prepared to make cosmetic changes must expect the same in return.

By July 2004, the public's dissatisfaction with the government's record on crime and its prevention had become too great to ignore, so Blair came up with one of his customary prevarications – the 'five-year plan'. The obvious gimmick of introducing such a time dependent strategy the year before a general election aside, this latest initiative promised to reduce overall crime levels by fifteen percent.

People do not want a return to old prejudices and ugly discrimination but do want rules, order and proper behaviour. They know there is such a thing as society. They want a society of respect. They want the society of responsibility. They want a community where the decent, law-abiding majority are in charge. Where those who play by the rules do well, and those who don't get punished.

Aside from the sheer arrogance of daring to talk of a society of 'respect' and a society of 'responsibility' only a week after the Butler report into the Iraq war demonstrated that Blair was capable neither of taking responsibility for his actions nor of treating those who opposed those actions with anything like respect, such a soundbite doesn't actually even mean anything. It is particularly difficult to take Blair seriously when he yearns for a society where '...those who play by the rules do well, and those who don't get punished'.

It is more surely the Prime Minister's fault than anyone else's in Britain that we currently live in a society where those who play by the rules get punished and those who don't do well. One need only think of the police chief fired for not passing on sensitive information about Ian Huntley at a time when to do so would have been unethical for an example of the government's treatment of those who play by the rules. Furthermore, the fact that a serial rapist could win the lottery in

August 2004 whilst still in prison shows how well those who don't play the rules can do.

Lofty, ambiguous, and, in such a context, meaningless terms like 'respect' and 'responsibility' are forever being churned out by New Labour as a rhetorical smokescreen that allows them to reject the very 'responsibilities' that the people voted them to take. The promise to cut crime by 15 per cent over the next five years is one that will doubtless be honoured, but it will be honoured in the government's usual manner of fiddling the figures and skewing the parameters of what is actually meant by 'cutting crime'.

The chances are that they will be able to prove that, in five years' time, they have cut crime by *more* than 15 per cent by citing the fact that society is no longer blighted by the outrageous activities of the criminal masterminds that used to be in operation; those who used to commit the cardinal sins of hunting with hounds, talking on their mobiles whilst driving, smoking in public places, smacking their children, voicing religious opinion, or accidentally stepping on harmless molluscs. Such slurs on the good name of society will by that time have been driven from the streets or locked away in prison. Tony Blair will be able to proudly claim, therefore, that 'crime' has been cut, and the fact that violent burglary and drug related murders will have exponentially risen over the same period will be neatly buried in the usual creative statistics.

It is a similar tactic employed by the naughty boy who, when told by his exasperated nanny to 'get to bed', replies cheekily that he *is* in bed, pulling a sheet over his body as he lies on the sofa to prove it, before continuing to watch cartoons on television. Such testing of authority is part of a growing up, and rather endearing. Similar behaviour on the part of a government is equally childish. However, it is not endearing, it is profoundly irresponsible.

The government's reorganisation of the legal system seems to be based on the model proposed by a character in a masterpiece of nonsense literature written over a hundred years ago. Its excuse for not tackling real crimes is that it is tackling the 'causes of crime' instead. This is a largely cosmetic shirking of its true duties, but perhaps the most damaging aspect of the Nanny State's incessant legislation and interference is that it necessarily forces people to redefine what is actually meant by 'crime'.

Naturally there are enormous and recognised differences in the gravity of crimes, but at least, until recently, there has been an acceptance that there is a difference between normal behaviour and criminal behaviour. Because this distinction is something that children can quickly understand, ideas of right and wrong, legal and illegal, can be relatively easily instilled.

However, how is anybody supposed to explain to a child, or indeed an adult, a justice system that considers both loving mothers issuing a light smack to discipline their offspring and violent rapists who murder and dismember their victims 'criminals'? The fact that the two 'crimes' would warrant very different punishment is not enough to escape the fact that, in such a system, the very nature of what is considered 'criminal' has been diluted, yet, in the moral climate that the government is attempting to create, responsibility of action is attached more strongly to those who commit petty offences than to those who do something seriously wrong.

Perhaps the Nanny State's most damaging legacy will be a diminution of the distinction between right and wrong. This is summed up by Judge Michael Hyam who said:

> History indicates that a proliferation of laws is an indication that a society is in bad health: when Parliament proceeds to deal with all the details of our daily lives there must inevitably be a great danger of law losing its moral sanction.

One would perhaps be forgiven for thinking that, given the government's 'proliferation of laws', 'Police State' might be a better description than 'Nanny State'. Despite the absurd quantity of new legislation that is constantly being passed, however, 'Police State' is not an accurate description, because there don't seem to be any policeman anywhere. There are hordes of traffic wardens, and police whose sole purpose seems to be catching motorists out for minor offences. There are also an increasing number of 'Community Support Officers' who essentially just help members of the public who are looking for directions. They are not equipped in any way to actually confront criminals, however, and there appear to be very few police who patrol the streets or spend their time dedicated to fighting crime like they do on television.

Partly, this is the fault of the spurious means by which the government achieves its beloved 'targets', but there is also another aspect to the pernicious influence of the Nanny State and the pointless reams of bureaucracy that it requires. The interference of the politically correct lobby has made a lot of genuine policing much more difficult. The MacPherson report into the Stephen Lawrence inquiry condemned the force as suffering from 'institutionalised' racism, while a necessary examination of the Metropolitan Police's methodology has created a counter-effect. The Met are now so bogged down with the paperwork deemed necessary so that any such future allegations can be properly investigated that many of them do not have time to be out on the streets actually tackling crime.

The other side of this coin is that, as well as being afraid of upsetting minorities when tackling crime, police work is now frequently tied up with the investigation of claims of such crimes as 'homophobia' and 'racism'. While such things are abhorrent, and society should strive to get rid of them, it is hardly a matter for the police to investigate. How can an irrational dislike of homosexuals, almost certainly based on a subconscious fear of one's own sexual orientation, be a police matter?

The much-derided 'thought police' are unfortunately no longer the stuff of fantasy. 'Crimes' which only occur in the mind cannot be prosecuted, but apparently can be 'investigated'. Such investigation will always be, however, a complete waste of time. The holding of unpleasant or untenable views cannot in itself be criminalised if isolated from actual criminal activity such as incitement to violence or racial hatred. Nor can 'wrongthinking' individuals be placed on the path of righteousness by a police investigation conducted by awkward bobbies who only became policemen because they enjoyed watching *Starsky and Hutch* as children. Indeed, skinhead idiots who pride themselves on their reputation as 'queerbashers' would no doubt leap to the characteristically ill-informed conclusion that the police themselves were queer for asking them about their sexual attitudes. This in turn would lead rather smartly to more 'queerbashing' of the hapless heterosexual bobbies, and hey presto, pointless time-wasting police procedure gives way to genuine, eminently avoidable criminal violence. The result is that there is no time in the working policeman's day to attend to the real crimes that take place in society. He is too busy obeying new legislative mandates more likely to engender than prevent crime.

Furthermore, it now seems to be accepted that offering the victims of crime 'counselling' is a valid alternative to either preventing or apprehending criminals. Beyond the offensiveness of assuming that all victims require counselling, and the arrogance of concluding that those who turn the 'offer' down are either in denial or a severe state of shock, is the problem of reputation.

Any institutionalised authority relies on society's respect for its survival. An element of fear may seem regrettable in our enlightened society, but without it the police are powerless. Imagine two burglars robbing a house suddenly hearing the wail of a siren. If their reaction is to say 'Don't worry, it's only the police' rather than to stop putting antiques into their swag bags immediately, the agents of law enforcement aren't even fighting a losing battle. They've actually lost. But the Nanny State's 'caring' attitudes towards law and order are reducing respect for the law and creating a worrying amount of disorder. They are also scaring the police themselves, further incapacitating them.

Whatever idealistic New Labour politicians may believe themselves, when they canvass for support in the run up to elections, they ignore the persistent demand that the council or government does something to sort out the crime problem. Local authorities seem to treat such requests as a complicated code, the true meaning of which is that the public want the government to crack down on speeding motorists, those who hunt foxes and those who smoke in public places. Some can even detect a clandestine plea on behalf of those who do not receive enough counselling after they have been subjected to more serious crime.

What people want is for real crime to be prevented, however, not a government that witters on about a society of 'respect' and 'responsibility', before demonstrating its refusal to take on any responsibility or show the electorate any respect.

7 Come with me, my pretties...

Maude Flanders: ' We're not talking about love, Edna. We are talking about S-E-X in front of the C-H-I-L-D-R-E-N!'

Krusty the Klown: '"Sex Cauldron!" I thought they shut that place down!'

The Simpsons Episode 172, 'Grade School Confidential'

If a traditional nanny does her job properly, the necessity for her employment diminishes as her charges grow older. In *Brideshead Revisited,* Sebastian Flyte may still have carried his teddy bear about with him at university, but he no longer required Nanny Hawkins to tend to his every need, and she retired to her room at Brideshead, surrounded by pictures of his childhood, where he would make certain to visit her whenever he could.

The Nanny State, however, is never prepared to accept that its job is done, and that its charges have grown up enough to fend for themselves, leading to the present situation where we have an adult population that will forever be treated like children. For that we have only ourselves to blame; after all, we were the ones that voted for these people, and we are the ones who continue to allow their authorised Nannies to boss us around. However, having given in to the government's insistence that we are incapable of looking after ourselves, we then have to accept their conclusion that we are incapable of looking after our children either. So we hand them over to the government for their upbringing and education.

It is here that an overbearing, controlling state can be seen to present the greatest danger. No longer does a child's understanding of the world develop through the teachings and values of its parents, but through the indoctrination of a set of ideas that the Nanny State believes to be inviolable. Such a nightmarishly Orwellian interpretation of the situation may seem overblown, but the ideas of New Labour are increasingly catching up with those of Big Brother. The schoolroom is the perfect testing ground for the more extreme examples of the Nanny State's experimentation, which they have no power to stop since like laboratory animals they do not have the vote.

Such an unfair legacy is one that our children simply do not deserve. Their childhoods are being robbed by a mean Nanny that refuses to let them go out and play, preventing them from exploring the world and making their own discoveries about it as children are supposed to. Instead, fears of rampant paedophiles and crazed motorists have put an end to lone bicycle rides or exploratory walks, and children are instead locked indoors in front of mind-wasting television programmes. Even when they are forced to go to school, there is little respite from their inertia because ludicrous Health and Safety measures have been introduced banning school trips or competitive play.

Once at school, there are fewer teachers than ever, most having been forced from that noble profession by the government's insulting pay packages and insistence that they only force on children its own blinkered political philosophy masquerading as education. The age at which this is set to begin is getting lower, as well, with the proposal that toddlers are forced into 'Sure Start' schools almost before they can walk, so that their absorbent minds can be filled with Tony Blair and his cronies' world view as early as possible. Children deserve to be left to make their own discovery of each other and the world precisely so that they can develop an objective opinion on them, guided but not brainwashed by their elders. In the very rare cases where parents abdicate their responsibility entirely, it is obviously necessary that some sort of state-sponsored mechanism is in place to pick up the pieces.

Most parents become so because they *want* children and, when they do, their love for them and desire to protect them is instinctive. Each generation, in general, strives to provide the best that they can for their offspring. Measures are required to prevent the abuse of children, certainly, but the idea that an entire ministry should be set up for their protection is nightmarishly totalitarian, and the idea of a 'Minister for Children' has echoes of the scary 'Child Catcher' in *Chitty Chitty Bang Bang* who takes naughty boys and girls away from their parents.

However badly they may have behaved, no child can possibly deserve to be represented by Margaret Hodge, who, in June 2003 (on Friday 13th) was appointed to the newly created post, and immediately set about cementing an image of a mean and scary nanny far more frightening than anything in literature.

Hodge, who had been Minister for Higher Education since 2001, tried to hit the ground running in her new post but immediately fell over with allegations of child abuse in an Islington care home under her leadership of the council. Initially she laughed off Demetrius Panton's claims of horrific abuse made in a televised documentary and described him as an 'extremely disturbed person' in a letter to the chairman of the BBC. The threat of legal action from Panton forced her to change her mind, however, and she instead agreed to pay £10,000 to his chosen charity.

With the irritating scandal aside, Hodge pressed ahead with the job in hand, addressing a conference jointly organised by *The Guardian*, *Community Care* magazine and the Association of Directors of Social Services. The terrifying title of the conference was 'Children – *Do They Count?*'. The suggestion that such a point might ever need debating is horrible enough, but the idea that the self-appointed guardians of the nation's children should consider it so is disgraceful. Aside from this, given Labour's contempt for its own 'Education, education, education' pledge, a better title for the conference might have been 'Children - *Can They Count?*'.

Hodge told the conference that she wished to tackle 'deprivation' in the private as well as the public sphere, 'by force' if necessary, and she praised the government's achievement of wishing to halve child poverty 'by 2010'. Such an intention is obviously laudable, even if praise for something the government 'hopes' to do is a little premature. However, she then stated that the definition of 'poverty' in this sense had been broadened to include 'poor parenting' and 'low aspirations'. Citing research which apparently showed parenting to be more important in the upbringing of a child than factors such as money or education, she added, with chilling sincerity:

> If parenting is so important, and has such an important
> impact on children, we *cannot* abandon it to the vagaries of
> the individual.'

The nasty sophistry of Hodge's rhetoric perfectly encapsulates the deluded and totalitarian mania that drives the nannying intentions of this government. They really do believe that the nation's children are theirs to be indoctrinated as they see fit, that parents are merely the means by which the children are produced. From such a position, bringing up children rightly becomes the preserve of the state.

St. Ignatius Loyola, the founder Jesuits, is regarded with hostility for saying, 'Give me a child for the first seven years, and you may do what you like with him afterwards.' His implication was that our formative years are so crucial to our development that we are essentially set for life by the time we reach the age of seven. New Labour may not seem at first glance to have much in common with the extremist Loyola, but the bottom line is the same when Hodge declares that '...good parenting has a greater influence on a child's education attainment level than any other factor'.

In fact, the government could rewrite the Jesuit maxim to describe their own aims very succinctly if they said, 'Give us a child for the first three years and we will so thoroughly confuse him that he will be incapable of fending for himself or leading a normal life afterwards.' The government is so convinced that the experiences of early childhood determine our entire future, a notion dubbed 'infant determinism', that they are not prepared to leave parenting in the hands of parents. If a parent gets it wrong in these first years, the child will be doomed to a fruitless, criminal, wasted life, and that is why we desperately need the help of Margaret Hodge and her Ministry for Children. They are convinced that infant determinism is an incontrovertible fact. Furthermore, the blithe assumption of the government is that they will never get it wrong.

The idea that our infancy dictates the course of our life was propagated by John Bowlby, a 1960s American child psychiatrist whose 'attachment theory' argued that the bond between child and parent in the first few months, when the brain is rapidly expanding, determined the child's future. This questionable theory had become accepted as a standard upon which to base US policy by 1997, when Hillary Clinton boldly stated that the first three years '...can determine whether children will grow up to be peaceful or violent citizens, focused or undisciplined workers, attentive or detached parents themselves'. The relative early childhoods and subsequent careers of Martin Luther King and Darius Guppy suggest a slightly more complicated story. These remain interesting points of debate, not empirical facts which governments can rely on, but that has not stopped New Labour from doing just that. The idea is particularly attractive to doctrinaire, idealistic politicians because it authorises them to conduct social experiments upon the most defenceless section of the community. New Labour are obsessed by 'chances'; by giving them, making sure people have them, ensuring they don't miss them or misuse them. Nothing excites them more than a theory which morally authorises them to interfere with the family to make certain that these 'chances' are taken. The New Labour pamphlet 'Every Child Matters' delivers with the weight of revelation the tired old cliché that '...the period from conception through to the start of school is crucial to later life chances'.

One wonders why they don't date the start of our 'life chances' even earlier, as Laurence Sterne's absurdist eighteenth-century masterpiece *Tristram Shandy* does, directly relating the formation of the hero's personality to the mood his parents were in the night they conceived him. Perhaps Blair's 'young Britain' doesn't have time for such old works, but more modern debunkings have had similarly little effect on Hodge and her followers. John Bruer is the author of *The Myth of the First Three Years* and is highly critical of those who peddle notions of 'crisis, of once-in-a-lifetime opportunities, and of use-it-or-lose-it developmental brinkmanship'. There is something deeply disturbing about the idea that we are set for life at such an early age, because it carries with it the implication that an 'unsuccessful' first stage of development will result in a 'bad' human being. Should those whom the government deem to have been poorly 'parented' be gathered up on their fourth birthday in a modern equivalent of King Herod's child policy and disposed of?

No one can say definitively what combination of factors shape the development of our lives and personalities because it is not a subject about which we can intelligently generalise. Not only are masses of children late developers but also the majority are far tougher than the government would like them to be. Quite apart from not realising that most parents can take charge of their own parenting, Hodge and Co. don't seem to have realised that a huge number of *children* can look after themselves. Infant determinists have to resort to extreme examples of child neglect to prove their case. In his book *They Fuck You Up*, Oliver James uses the damage done to abandoned children raised by wild animals to prove the importance of 'total parenting'. But as Dr Helene Guldberg, a child development lecturer, points out, 'James seems to forget that very few of us are raised by wolves. There is a world of difference between being completely starved of human contact and having parents who do not measure up to James's standards.'

If they are brought up in a normal, stable environment, most babies will develop through interaction with the world around them, notwithstanding the whale noises piped into their tiny ears at birth, or how much Beethoven their parents play them in the womb. At the other end of the scale, says Steve Petersen, a neuroscientist at Washington University, it takes a very bad environment to interfere with development. He too has advice for parents, but of a slightly more sensible sort than Margaret Hodge: 'Don't raise your child in a closet, starve them, or hit them on the head with a frying pan.' The current embrace of such fatalistic philosophies as infant determinism feeds on the pernicious belief that people cannot live their lives without professional guidance, especially when it comes to something as important as parenting. Calling the creed of infant determinism into question may upset perfectionist parents who dream of creating a little genius, but is crucial in order to prevent both them and their offspring from experiencing lifelong feelings of guilt and inadequacy.

In their bid to get control of children's minds as early as possible, Labour have concentrated particularly on their project of playgroup expansion. David Blunkett somewhat disingenuously stated in 2000 that 'it is, of course, up to parents of under-fives to decide what they think best for their children, and they may choose not to take a nursery or playgroup place.' As if the government's unsought opinion were not already abundantly clear, he went on to say that

> We are making this investment because we want formal nursery education, from three onwards, to become as much a part of bringing up children as primary and secondary school are today. I appeal to parents to take their responsibilities seriously and think what is best for their child – what will help them best begin the process of learning and play, and how important it is for them to arrive at primary school with the confidence and social skills needed to make a good start.

In other words, it isn't really up to parents to decide what is best for the under-fives after all, because New Labour have already decided that they should be firmly enrolled in a Sure Start Primary School by the time they are three.

It is risible, given how much authority the government is taking for infant education, that Blunkett can say that

> Education is a partnership in which parents have a critical role. We want them to engage much more in the education of their children than in the past. And with the investment we are now making in universal under-five provision, there is no longer any need to wait until five or even four before building the partnership between parents and teachers which is so crucial to a child's success.

The 'partnership' being proposed constitutes huge fines and even incarceration for parents who fall foul of the government's standards. Estelle Morris's claim that New Labour is merely helping parents to become better parents is both arrogant and untrue. New Labour are marginalising parents as far as possible in order to pursue hopeless social experiments in the name of 're-education'.

The professional 're-education' on offer is in the hands of people like Dr. Pat Preedy, who has written a step-by-step guide to infant fitness which will be taught at all Sure Start centres in the country. Mothers will be told how to help their toddlers to rock, grasp, sit up, crawl and balance with the help of the lottery-funded manual, which has, alas, come too late to educate the millennia of parents who have had to bring up their babies without it.

Preedy, a former head teacher, said that her advice to parents was necessary – Nannies always claim their prescriptions are necessary – because 'modern living' meant that children were less active and had fewer opportunities to crawl around on the floor. She stated:

With the use of baby walkers and bouncers and specially designed chairs, babies do not crawl and explore as much as they used to,' she said. 'They are therefore missing out on much-needed physical exercise and sensations. Because of sudden infant death syndrome we now tend to lie babies on their back. They then have less opportunity to push themselves up and develop their neck muscles. Even something like the thick-soled shoes we now put on very young children can hamper their ability to balance, which is initially based on sensing through their feet.

A gross and totally unsupported assumption is being made here about the lifestyles of millions of parents and children based on the opinions of a handful of predominantly urban childminders. Clearly, some infants do not get enough exercise, but to pressurise, and ultimately legislate, society as a whole to put its children into Sure Start Primary Schools is an outrageous abuse of authority. Law-abiding, responsible parents who live nowhere near one of these centres will be besieged with worry and doubt about their efficacy as a parent if they do not make the huge effort to enrol their children.

The introduction of the exercise routine was prompted by research at the Institute of Neuro-Physiological Psychology in Chester, which found that physical movement was essential to a child's brain development. Researchers found that children who grow up without experiencing the full range of movements are at a neuro-physical disadvantage that limits their ability to learn.

Preedy, who is now the head of research and development with Global Education Management Systems, a company that runs independent schools, said that the new booklet offered a range of 'keep fit' options.

Among them are a series of drawings and photographs showing parents how to rock their newborns up and down and forward and back, as well as from side to side. Presumably these are the sorts of actions Preedy does not trust parents to work out for themselves. The wheelbarrow movement involves moving the baby's legs towards and away from the adult, in a process far too complicated to attempt without Preedy's instructions. Mothers are told to play roly-poly by placing a toy next to the child and helping it to roll over and back, another brain-busting complex manoeuvre without a manual to assist you. Other exercises place babies on their stomachs and help them lift up into a crouching position in readiness to crawl. Using a small ball, children are encouraged to develop their pincer grip, which is essential for eventually holding a pencil at school. It is not yet known how many children to date have been ridiculed on their first day at school because they didn't attend a Sure Start centre and therefore don't know how to pick up a pencil.

Dr Preedy had no time for claims that the booklet was preaching to parents and giving advice on activities that came naturally. 'The nine parents who tested the movements thought it was great. It helped them when they realised the point of what they were doing.' It is a point most people would take a very long time to 'realise', but Preedy claims that '…I wish there had been something like this around when I was a young mum'. Margaret Morrissey, the spokesman for the National Confederation of Parent Teacher Associations, said that parents should be encouraged to develop movement in their babies, but warned that they should not feel guilty if they do not slavishly follow a routine. 'The message needs to be supportive. The last thing we need is a stressed mother of three worrying that they are going to fail at school because she didn't have time to go through an exercise regime.'

It is abundantly clear that the government doesn't intend to let parents rear their offspring unaided in their first few crucial years of development. The lunacy does not stop there, however. Once children have been taught how to crawl, clutch, chuckle and gurgle by New Labour, there is a horrifying possibility that they may take advantage of their newfound knowledge and misbehave. At this stage, it really is up to parents to discipline children hitherto brought up by Tony Blair. After all, Jack Straw claims that '...government is not about lecturing people about the way they should live their lives'. Estelle Morris goes further, admitting that '...the state is not a good parent'. Unfortunately though, she goes on to contradict herself, saying that:

> A message has gone to the child that teachers should not be respected and adults should not be respected, and that's not good enough...It's not easy for politicians to raise these issues. But we need to break that taboo – if children continue to misbehave and parents aren't carrying out their responsibilities, then something needs to be done. The tide must be turned.

Her intention to intervene in children's discipline when parents fail in their duties persists despite the findings of December 2000 when the Department for Education & Employment published the results of its own opinion poll. Eighty-four per cent of parents believed that they and not the state should have the right to decide whether a parent should be permitted to smack their child. Only 10 per cent thought the state should impose its own view on the matter. In response to the survey, while Secretary of State for Education, David Blunkett stated that:

> I do believe that the right to smack in exceptional circumstances is one which should remain with parents and with childcarers who are carrying out the explicit wishes of parents.... This is one issue where the role of government and the state should not be extended into people's homes. It should be for parents to decide for themselves.

If you can work your way through the morass of contradictions espoused by two successive New Labour Education Secretaries, it seems that Morris's government wants to discipline children itself but Blunkett's believes that '...it should be for parents to decide for themselves'. It is no surprise that such confusion has been a breeding ground for nannying organisations with their own pointless agendas. The lead agency of the anti-smacking lobby group is punchily called 'Children are Unbeatable!' and it is gathering power at an alarming rate in Westminster.

Sure Start Minister Baroness Ashton revealed that childminders who smack a minded child, no matter how mildly, would be guilty of a criminal offence under new regulations due to come into force in September, 2004, even where physical correction has been authorised by the child's parent. This legislation will be a preliminary to removing 'smacking privileges' from parents themselves as well. In response to an enquiry from national advocacy group 'Families First', Lady Ashton stated that offending childminders would be required to attend 'behaviour management training' in the first instance, followed by prosecution or 'other enforcement action' if they persisted in smacking. Norman Wells of 'Families First' commented:

> It is outrageous that a government minister should presume to dictate to parents how their children may or may not be reasonably disciplined when entrusted to the care of a childminder. Lady Ashton is flying in the face of common sense and of a public opinion poll commissioned by her own department, which shows that 84 per cent consider this to be a matter that can be left with parents and childminders to agree between themselves. Without a shred of evidence in support of its position, the department seems to have made up its mind that smacking is the worst thing a childminder can do to a child, when all the research evidence demonstrates that physical correction used consistently and with care in the context of a stable and secure relationship is an effective form of discipline. This draconian measure undermines both parents and childminders, many of whom have successfully brought up children of their own with the use of judicious physical correction, and runs counter to the principles of the Children Act 1989 which provides that parents may arrange for some or all of their responsibilities to be met by another

person acting on their behalf. It also stigmatises parents who use physical correction in the discipline of their own children and suggests that their care is substandard and unprofessional.

Mr. Wells might be even more incensed if he knew what organisations like 'Children are Unbeatable!' are using in lieu of 'evidence'.

The organisation shrilly states that 'Children are being legally hit right now!' as if the sound of children being brutally disciplined were as commonplace as birdsong or the roar of traffic. In fact, its entire argument is based on one piece of extremely questionable research carried out by two child psychologists in 1997 commissioned by the Department of Health. 'Children are Unbeatable!' asserts that the study was based on interviews with more than four hundred families, but the key findings were drawn from a sample group of less than a hundred families, whose 'nationally representative' status is somewhat undermined by the fact that they all come from the same health authority list in a district of South London. Unbeatable!'s terrifying claim that '...over ninety per cent of parents hit and most children are hit and many are hit severely' is unsupportable as a global extrapolation of a tiny sample of less than a hundred families. They are using such misleading statistics to remove the defence of 'reasonable chastisement' from the Statute Book, where it has been since 1860, when Lord Chief Justice Cockburn ruled that '...by the law of England, a parent may, for the purpose of correcting what is evil in the child, inflict moderate and reasonable corporal punishment'. That this is often the reason that police do not feel able to prosecute child abusers is clearly wrong, but the proposed solution would be even worse. Baroness Findlay of Llandaff, on behalf of 'Children are Unbeatable!', addressed the House of Lords in May 2004 with an impassioned story:

> I know what it is like to be lonely, living in a highrise block with no money and two babies, one of whom cries incessantly. Without the restraint of having worked in paediatrics and having seen the results of shaking and hitting, I would have lost my rag. I feared that once I hit I would have been unable to stop, such was the pent-up emotion that I felt. That was as a young mum. The purpose of this reform is to send clear and unequivocal messages to parents that assaulting children, like assaulting adults, is wrong and unlawful.

The Baroness appears to miss her own point here. The reason she gives for not hitting her children is that she had seen the results of abuse, not that a government had sent her a 'clear and unequivocal message' that it was wrong. Furthermore, having ended up a Baroness in the Lords, she is clearly far from typical of desperate single mothers, however much 'pent-up emotion' she felt. She is typical of New Labour in mistakenly assuming that her personal experience qualifies her to legislate for others with whom she has almost nothing in common.

Arrogance is not the worst problem that state interference with family discipline highlights. Findlay assured the House that a change to the law would not create a new offence; it would only remove a cruel, outdated defence. She also vowed that the amendment, as drafted, would not result in increased prosecutions of parents for minor incidents. If that were true, no one in their right mind would object to the proposal. It is patently and necessarily not true, however, and nor could it possibly be. The amendment, whether it removed a defence or created an offence, would result in a ban on smacking, and the DPP have stated that inevitably '...even minor assaults would be criminalised'. Smacking cannot be banned unless you are prepared to prosecute people who continue to smack. The removal from parents of the right to 'reasonably chastise' their own children will criminalise millions of loving, responsible parents who slap a naughty child. It would be illogical to tell parents that they are criminals if they smack but that they will be let off if they are guilty. The police would be forced to assess individual 'smacks' before deciding whether they were serious enough to merit prosecution or not. If that becomes the case, our legal system will become even more ridiculous than New Labour's 'reforms' have made it so far. The law may always have been 'an ass', but under the present government it is an ass with terrible incontinence.

Heavily funded campaigns like 'Children are Unbeatable!' and the anti-hunting movement never go away. Once they enter the body politic they course around Westminster clogging up the system fruitlessly, whether they ever become law or not. If this one does, all parents who decide, for whatever reason, that the best way to put a stop to a child's misbehaviour is a smack or who have the misfortune to lose their temper, as even the most reasonable parent might from time to time, will have committed a crime. Their children will be able to report them to the police, and then they will be put on some infernal list, and social services will be informed, and certain jobs will cease to be available to them, and they will be stigmatised...the chain of events set in motion could be catastrophic for the hitherto law-abiding citizen.

The change to the law will fundamentally change the legal relationship between a parent and a child, and will encourage children to believe, both at home and at school, that they have a right to behave as they please and have no obligation to follow adult instruction or direction, just as children at school do not believe that they have any duty to respect the teachers standing in front of them. Estelle Morris claims that the government should be '...about supporting a parent to be a better parent...', but then her idea of 'parental support' lies in encouraging children not to respect the discipline of their parents.

As spanking has been made more difficult in the extremely rights-conscious United States ('Spanking hurts everybody!' scream lobbyist billboards), the use of the behaviour-suppressant drug Ritalin has soared. Children are either out-of-control little Bash Street Kids who need more discipline, or they're pilled-up, listless zombies like the Midwich Cuckoos. Nowhere is any allowance made for them to just be children. Furthermore, lawless, violent parents, those largely responsible for child violence in the first place, will continue to hit children regardless of new legislation. After all, if laws were reliable preventatives, then we would not have the war on drugs.

One mother's response to Baroness Findlay's amendments was

> I'm furious about it. I don't go about whacking my children,
> but I do believe a calm premeditated slap, given after a
> warning, can draw the line under particularly buggersome
> behaviour. If smacking was banned, I'd feel despair, and even
> more marginalised as a parent than I do already.

Once children have been taught how to crawl by the government, combating the severe disability imposed by evil 'thick-soled shoes', and have been protected from cruel parents who want to 'legally hit' them, it is time for them to go to school.

The British school system is a perfect model for all that is misguided, unhelpful, anti-social and sometimes actually dangerous about Nanny Statism. It brings together most of Blair's preoccupations in a single institution, where health regulations mix freely with child-rearing, elitism, sex, incivility, obesity and, occasionally, education in one big socially experimental arena. Under New Labour, schools appear to function far less as places to teach children than as sites for the working out of rival social doctrines. Blair's infamous 'Education, education, education' electoral pledge was instantly exposed as nonsense when he introduced tuition fees almost as soon as he became Prime Minister, but the universities are not where the real damage is being done. After all, New Labour cannot be blamed for a tertiary education system that has been consistently ridiculed for decades. They should, however, be blamed for making it worse.

Kingsley Amis was complaining as long ago as 1960 about that:

> The delusion that there are thousands of young people
> about who are capable of benefiting from university
> training, but have somehow failed to find their way there,
> is a necessary component of the expansionist case. More
> will mean worse.

Margaret Hodge sees it differently, claiming that New Labour's expansionist policies are 'firmly rooted in our analysis of the labour market needs – all too often our plans for expansion are misunderstood, are subject to derision or are at their worst vehemently attacked.'

Hodge clearly does not consider the availability of degree courses on Manchester United or 'gameshow analysis' a 'devaluing of traditional higher education'. She actually sounded hurt in a speech in November 2002 when she complained:

> We are accused of deliberately dumbing down academic
> standards and we are accused of killing off the supply of
> skilled tradesmen in one fell swoop. Nothing could be
> further from the truth.

Despite the fact that New Labour's target of fifty per cent of young people entering tertiary education necessitates the invention of a massive quantity of new courses, Hodge insisted that '...raising ambitions among more young people and raising achievement levels among more young people does not imply devaluing the currency of a degree'. She scoffed at the idea that numbers should be 'artificially capped to maintain the integrity of the degree' saying such thinking represented the 'prejudices of those who want to protect a social elite rather than the ambitions of those who want to build an intellectual majority'. The simplistic polarisation of 'prejudice' and 'ambition' is totally misleading, and characteristic of everything the government does. There is no way to make a vast increase in the amount of degree courses available without 'devaluing the currency of a degree' because the essence of a degree is that it distinguishes its holder from those who don't have one. Gold is more valued than coal because it is scarcer. This is not 'good' or 'bad'. It's just true. The only way to get fifty percent of young people into tertiary education is by creating courses that no previous government, Conservative or Labour, would have considered worth taking. New Labour are institutionalising the kind of irresponsible parenting that sees children pushed unwillingly into areas they are unsuited to by their ambitious parents. Hodge defends the government's position with the unbelievably clumsy counter-argument that '...we are skilling up our population, not dumbing down'. Furthermore, apparently 'eight out of ten jobs now require the skills and competences which can only be gained through higher education'. Even Hodge must know this is completely untrue, or the government would be morally obliged to set a target of eighty per cent university attendance, rather than their proposed fifty.

Warning signs have been there ever since the publication of Peter Mandelson and Roger Liddle's work *The Blair Revolution: Can New Labour Deliver?* New Labour are obsessed with raising 'standards' in state schools, which are funded by the government. It would be reasonable to assume that the most a responsible government can do is effectively raise and distribute money to tackle specific problems.

Unless ministers have the time to go into schools and actually start teaching children personally it is hard to see what else they can usefully do. Creating legislation which unconsulted teachers then have to enforce whether they like it or not is the New Labour way to raise 'standards', however. 'Each child should have his or her own individual learning plan devised by the teacher and reviewed with a parent at regular six-monthly meetings attendance at which would be a new legal requirement...' opines Mandelson. 'Where a parent failed to meet this obligation, this would be prima facie evidence of a child at risk of educational failure.'

Mandelson also believes that...

> Schools require a new, much tougher set of disciplinary sanctions to deal with unruly and uncooperative pupils, such as compulsory homework on school premises, weekend and Saturday night detentions, and the banning of favourite leisure pursuits such as attendance at football matches.

Whilst he is completely wrong to describe Saturday detention as a 'new' idea, it is indeed both 'new' and totally unworkable to try and stop naughty children from attending 'favourite leisure pursuits'. Since the majority of these proposals were dreamt up to make up for the supposed failures of parenting, it is rather self-defeating to create legislation which relies on co-operation between school and, er, parents. It is worth noting that 'leisure' only exists in the New Labour world view as something to be taken away from naughty people. The systematic implementation of Mandelson's educational dream has been exacerbated in recent years not only by Estelle Morris's total incompetence, but by her predecessor David Blunkett's draconian refusal to let reality interfere with his policies. The crucial question getting buried deeper and deeper beneath all this state interference is why the government thinks it has the right to tell teachers and parents how to treat their children in the first place.

New Labour lost no time in pointing out that their educational policies would 'benefit the many, not just the few' in their White Paper *Excellence in Schools* published in July 1997. 'This will inevitably mean smaller classes, more equitable funding and fairer admissions,' it claimed, although it unbelievably also stated that schools would get new funds for repairs and maintenance only if they could show they were 'improving standards'. The simultaneous naming, authorised by Blunkett, of the 'eighteen worst schools in the country' did not have any immediately obvious benefits either to the many or the few. It did humiliate some already struggling institutions, however, and further reduce their initiative or ability to work through their funding difficulties. It must have been difficult to believe that the new government was committed to improving 'standards' if you worked in one of those eighteen schools, whose problems were made immeasurably worse by such iniquitous finger-pointing. As has so often been the case, the only real change New Labour's attentions resulted in were cosmetic. The attempt to re-brand comprehensive schools as 'post-comprehensive' did not work, so a think tank of some originality decided to stick with what it knew, and persuaded many schools to start referring to themselves as 'new comprehensives'. Other pointless euphemisms include 'fresh start schools', which are failing schools given a new name to stop the same names constantly appearing at the bottom of the league tables, 'schools in special measures', which are essentially the same thing as 'fresh start schools', 'city academies', which are privately-financed schools where profits are a more important consideration than education, and 'training schools', which are schools where pupils are taught by unqualified teachers. Perhaps best of all is the description of 'schools in special measures', which are defined privately as schools failing too obviously for the government to get away with calling them 'fresh start schools'.

In terms of practical educational improvement, this kind of time-wasting verbiage is all New Labour is capable of, unless you count Mandelson's book. David Blunkett crowed in 2000:

> Where schools have been failing, we've taken action. Over five hundred failing schools have come off special measures since 1997. Others have been closed or given a fresh start. Sometimes we might need to do even more, because turning around a failing school is never easy! City academies will offer new hope too where inner city schools have been failing.

Once one translates the euphemisms into English, it rapidly becomes apparent that what Blunkett actually means is that the government has done absolutely nothing. In the realm of damaging, unwarranted interference, on the other hand, it has made enormous strides since 1997.

David Blunkett told the New Labour Party Conference in 2000:

> We're putting modernisation into practice. We're building
> the schools of the future, where the needs of every child are
> met and the talents of every child are fully developed.
> Schools where there is the support and the equipment to do
> the job. An education system where children learn the
> basics and are therefore able to access the wider
> curriculum. One where we've given parents a greater voice
> than ever before – and opened up the curriculum to them in
> ways no government has ever previously done.

Beyond the irony of a government which has marginalised
parents like never before claiming to have given them 'a greater voice
than ever before', Blunkett's speech said absolutely nothing about
how any of this would actually *happen.* It is indicative of the nanny
to fuss and oversee without ultimately assuming responsibility and
one of the great diseases of New Labour is the prefererence for
activity over effectiveness. Inevitably it is our schools which suffer
most from the need of the Government to be seen to be doing
something. Schools were the main victims of Blunkett's itch to
intervene: when he was Education Secretary it resulted in a teaching
profession that was crippled with the onslaught on directives from his
department. Things did not changed under either Morris or Clarke.
Seventy different consultation and instruction documents have
arrived in schools over the past year, many of them with absurdly
short response times, allowing Governors and teachers no chance of
a considered reaction. One headmaster, when asked whether all this

paper was distracting his staff, said it had no effect, good or bad, because '...I throw it all in the bin as soon as it arrives'. This is an understandable reaction, but it suggests that the government's complacent belief in educational improvement has no basis in reality.

Another of Blunkett's claims was that:

> We are equipping our nation for a world of tomorrow. We are modernising and reforming for a purpose. Our job is to ensure that every school is a good school – that the roof doesn't leak, that the heating works, that the children are warm. That temporary classrooms are replaced, that schools are refurbished.

A government that boasts of its intention to 'equip' the nation for a 'world of tomorrow' (what other sort of world could we possibly prepare for?) needs concrete policies to back up its idealism, but Blunkett seemed keener on further waffle. It is hard to make any sense whatsoever of the proclamation that 'Excellence in cities is central to raising standards in the most disadvantaged areas!'. Only Californian potheads like Bill and Ted in their Excellent Adventure think that 'excellence' is a tangible, meaningful goal that can be realised by saying 'Excellent!' the whole time.

Another area in which the nannies of the state have extended their unwelcome intrusion into the schooling system is in Health and Safety. The need to protect citizens from danger is clearly a government responsibility. It would even be possible to defend a government which carried out its duties over-zealously in the interests of national security, if it had the full support of its people. The logical end point of New Labour's attitude towards our safety, however, can be seen in the case of little Georgia Holt, a ten-year-old pupil at Seymour Road Primary School, in Clayton, Greater Manchester. During a particularly hot weekend in July 2003, her mother responsibly administered sun protection lotion to her. The heatwave showed no signs of abating as the school week began, so Georgia took the sunscreen to school, where she was barred from applying it for fear that her classmates might share it and have an allergic reaction. This was despite the advice of experts such as Nicola O'Connor, of Cancer Research UK, who said that '...the risk of being burnt far outweighs the risk of a minor allergy'.

Furthermore, Dr Juliette Loncaster, a skin cancer consultant at Christie Hospital, Manchester, warned that '...excessive sun exposure, and particularly sunburn, when aged under 15 is a major risk factor for cancer in later life'. Georgia's mother, Wendy, a carer herself, could only fume:

> It's absolutely ridiculous. I don't know what the school is thinking of. Do they not care about the health and safety of pupils? When I rang the school they said I could come along a couple of times in the day and apply lotion to Georgia, but I work.

Unsurprisingly, the school itself refused to comment on its ridiculous ruling, but seemed steadfast in its determination not to reconsider. A spokesman for Manchester city council said the decision was in line with its health and safety policies:

> Parents are encouraged to apply a high factor sun screen to
> their children before they leave for school and to send them
> to school wearing loose fitting clothing and a sun hat. We
> advise that children do not bring sunscreen into school, or
> share it with other children, as some children can suffer
> allergic reactions.

Dr. Loncaster could only speak from deadly experience in vain when she warned that '...applying sunscreen before school will unfortunately not provide adequate protection all day'. Mrs. Holt told local journalists that '...there are all these warnings telling you to wear sunscreen. All I've tried to do is make my daughter aware from an early age'.

Unfortunately, the local council, with the full support of the government, has more authority over children's health and safety than fully qualified cancer specialists. A cynic might surmise that local authorities run more risk of civil action from the parents of a child who can prove that he or she suffered an allergic reaction at school than from parents of a child who contracts skin cancer, a disease of untraceable provenance.

Such decisions, and the fact that the propaganda put about by the Nanny State has begun to affect the judgement of parents, means that the playground is an ever more sanitised environment in which bored little children walk around in circles because the swings have been removed and ball games have been banned because they encourage dangerous 'competitiveness'. At the same time, parents who have been rendered incapable of rational thought by their own submission to the Nanny State, chauffeur their children from the door of their homes to the school gates, so terrified are they of the threat of paedophilic madmen, and then ring to complain if they see their little darlings playing outside in the cold or the rain.

Diane Rich, of the British Association for Early Childhood Education, believes that such a cloistered existence, beyond merely boring children and stunting the development of their relationship to the world, is actually physically harmful for children, as it depresses the immune system, stunts the development of muscles and hampers balance and coordination skills. 'Recent research even shows that lack of fresh air can deprive the growing brain of oxygen and impair cognitive development,' she told the *Telegraph* in March 2004.

No doubt the government-encouraged sedentary and housebound lifestyles of children is itself responsible for the fact that children are getting fatter. The prospect of legislation which aims to protect children's health directly contradicting legislation designed to protect children's safety cannot be far away.

The 'Early Childhood Education' association became so concerned about the prison-like existence that was being imposed on children, that they published a book, *The Great Outdoors*, to try to encourage children to abandon their televisions and computer games and venture outside.

There is little chance that her laudable aim will be achieved, however, even in those schools which still have playing fields on which the children can play, because once there the children have had the fun of outdoor games removed by yet more nannying.

In Edinburgh, the council have decreed that, in the spirit of 'fairness' and 'inclusion', the score in school football games must be levelled to nil-nil at half time. Also, where one team is ahead by more than three goals, the losing team is allowed to take on two extra players. What the point of this is, other than taking the excitement out of the game, and failing to teach children how to lose with good grace, is a mystery.

In a particularly unfunny moment during his autobiography, *On a Clear Day*, David Blunkett tells of a visit he made as Secretary of Education to a primary school. Ushered into a school classroom full of infants, he sat on one of the tiny child's chairs. His knees level with his chin, he put his arm around the occupant of the next chair and, in what he calls 'my most soothing politician's voice' he asked: 'And how old are you, my dear?' 'Twenty-three,' replied the startled nursery teacher.

This was an especially ironic moment, however, because the former education secretary sanctioned policies that genuinely do treat primary school children as if they are years older than they are. Compulsory sex education for five-year-olds was one of New Labour's inspirationally misguided innovations, which Blunkett pioneered. Under intense pressure from the Independent Advisory Group on Teenage Pregnancy, the government was determined to try almost anything to reduce the under-eighteen conception rate.

'More confident' teaching of personal, social and health education (or PSHE) to five-year-olds is required, the government-appointed group claimed.

Gill Frances, deputy chairwoman of the advisory group, complained that the subject...

> ...is not properly assessed across all schools. It is important
> to start education about sex and relationships in the early
> years at primary school. Encouraging children to start
> talking about feelings and relationships develops emotional
> skills that help them to avoid teenage pregnancy, sexually
> transmitted infection and drug taking.

Such concepts may be plain baffling to the average five-year-old, but the group has advised ministers to give statutory force to sex education guidelines they have prepared. Apparently, children need to understand 'the need for love in stable relationships and the safe routines needed to avoid the spread of viruses including HIV.' By the age of five. Ms Frances wisely conceded that '...there is no point in pushing schools to do more than parents and the local community can stand.' Presumably this is why the age at which children *must* understand how to avoid catching AIDS is not two or three. If a lone cranky parent wished to confuse its child with so much sophisticated information at five, it would be considered very odd, perhaps even bad parenting. But when the government removes from parents the right to protect their children from premature exposure to these sensitive ideas it is presented as a moral imperative from a state that knows better than the individual.

The organisation 'Added Power and Understanding in Sex Education' or APAUSE is a government-backed body that urges young people to avoid having penetrative sex by discussing alternative levels of intimacy such as oral sex. Family campaigners particularly object to its attempts to curb unwanted pregnancy by teaching schoolchildren about the alternative joys of anal sex and gay sex. Robert Whelan, of the Family Education Trust, confined his comments to saying:

> It's regrettable that they put in the bit about oral sex for avoiding pregnancy. I don't think it's going to be effective at preventing teenage pregnancy. Most people are not terribly disciplined. When you are an adolescent your hormones are raging. Once you start you are going to go all the way.

John Rees, APAUSE's president, has no time for such common sense. He believes the programme, developed by researchers at Exeter University, 'empowers' young people and helps them to make 'informed choices' which will not, presumably, adversely affect their 'life chances'.

Obviously some sort of sex education is necessary so that the dangers of sexually transmitted diseases and unwanted pregnancies can be avoided, but to pretend that randy teenagers are going to make 'informed choices' which override the influence of their raging hormones is hopelessly naïve, as is the idea that discussing sex 'openly' with mixed classes of pubescent schoolchildren is going to elicit anything more fruitful than sniggers from the back of the class. It is in areas such as this that the Nanny State demonstrates a disturbing level of prurience. The proponents of groups such as A PAUSE come across less like a nanny and more like an embarrassing uncle who gets drunk at Christmas and asks girls if they have got their leg over yet and boys if they've tried their first joint.

Sexual discovery is necessarily embarrassing, painful, smelly and, occasionally, ends in disaster, however, it is also an intensely private process and essential to growing up. Therefore it is the job of teachers to detachedly inform pupils of the risks, but otherwise have nothing to do with it.

While children must to a certain extent be protected, they must also be allowed to make their own mistakes in life. Adults involved in looking after children must accept that they are never going to reclaim their own childhoods, and not try to live vicariously through those in their charge. There is a necessary distance that must be kept between teachers and their pupils, but it is a respectful one. It is a grave mistake to break that respect by encouraging teachers to disingenuously pretend to be the 'equals' of their pupils, or worse, by encouraging the teachers to become the policemen of their pupils – such as the government's unforgivable proposal that teachers should force pupils who behave suspiciously to be submitted to dehumanising and intrusive drug tests.

Teachers should be free to actually educate children, rather than have their time wasted with the various social experiments of a controlling government. Conversely, children should be allowed to *learn* about life. The Nanny State will never allow for this, however, as it instead pursues its own agenda, sanctioned by the apparent apathy of the children's parents, aimed at ridding them of the enormous joys, and necessary pains, that come from discovering the world for themselves.

Children should be seen and not heard

'Like the blind leading the blind, the ruler is like the ruled.'

Saint Jerome

This book was written in an office on the corner of a busy London crossroad which has the usual traffic lights plus *five* pelican crossings for pedestrians. As part of his one-Mayor's war against the motorcar Ken Livingstone has recently introduced a pedestrian crossing that traverses the road diagonally, which is why there is one more than the conventional four. When the road traffic lights turn to red, the pedestrian lights turn to green to signal that it is safe to cross. Many years ago this method of protecting people at crossings was complemented by a matronly female voice, announcing that it was 'safe' to cross. This was introduced because a purely visual signal discriminated against and endangered the blind.

A few years later, it was realised that this improved system still did not address the needs of blind foreign pedestrians. Pedestrian

Traffic Control commissioned the best brains in the field of road accidents involving blind foreign tourists to research the problem and write a report. They recommended, and this was accepted and implemented, that pelican crossing should now broadcast a non-verbal sound to signal to pedestrians when it was safe to cross the road. The sound that was selected for this most vital of duties – saving the lives of blind foreign pedestrian – was an automated equivalent of Bernard Herrmann's stabbing violin score from *Psycho*. Thus, the pelican crossing outside Artnik's office plays a piercing screech that pulses out for fifteen seconds every two minutes or so, hammering the aural equivalent of an icepick into the head of everyone who lives or works within fifty metres of the junction. It never stops...even into the early hours of the morning, when there are no pedestrians at all, never mind visually impaired ones, trying to cross the road.

No civilised society should be unmindful of the needs of its blind foreign pedestrians. But without a braille User's Guide by the roadside how are the beneficiaries of this particular facility supposed to know that the pelican screech means *Go* rather than *Wait*? And even if some progressive multiculturist Pedestrian Safety Officer, with special remit to assist the handicapped manages to procure the funding to install roadside instructions in braille, how would the blind know they were there?

There is also a problem with the type sound these devices emit. It is rather similar to the cry of a sentinel monkey warning the troop that there is a predator in the vicinity. It, therefore, appeals to our most atavistic instincts as a sign of danger rather than safety.

Combined with the frequency of the bleeping, if you were blind you could be forgiven for thinking that silence means it is safe to cross. Consequently, if the visually impaired took a blind bit of notice of these things, it could be the death of them.

If our progressive Pedestrian Safety Officer was alerted to this possibility, he would certainly address the issue. Perhaps inspired by the London Underground's stentorian 'Mind the Gap' warning, every time the doors open, which must have saved even more Londoners' lives than the pelican screech, he would go back to the spoken warning.

But this time the warning would be recorded in German as the streets of Battersea, where Artnik is located, are packed with blind German pedestrians. Of course, this would confuse blind English pedestrians who would need instruction in German to appreciate the difference between *Geen* and *Nicht zu geen*?... It is only by considering the mind-boggling philosophical complexities faced by the Nanny State apparatchiks, as they slave away on our behalf, that we can appreciate why they need to be paid so much.

In fact, anyone carrying a white stick or with a guide dog, who was uncertain how to get from one side of a road to the other, would be helped by a sighted pedestrian. Ordinary people actually do go out of their way to help someone who is handicapped and in difficulty. A measure of this disposition to help others can be seen, on the pavements of London, where young, fully able-bodied beggars can scrounge enough to feed a drug habit. On the whole, if people are given the chance, they are quite decent to each other.

It would be salutary experience for our hypothetical Pedestrian

Safety Officer to take a week off to observe his pelican crossing outside Artnik's office. He would not see one blind pedestrian relying on this device to cross the road. In fact, he would not see one blind person, German or otherwise. When one of the senses crash, such as sight, the body tries to compensate by heightening the performance of other senses such as hearing. Thus the awful sound at this roadside crossing makes blind people feel like they're being trepanned, which is why they avoid it like the plague.

Welcome to the Nanny State. It treats us all, effectively as if we are blind foreigners, unable to make our way about the world without screaming electronic bleeps and hideous 'Warning' signs everywhere.

The pelican screech embodies all the characteristics of the Nanny State. It does not do what it claims to do. It wastes money and employs people, in its installation and maintenance, in utterly useless tasks. But Nanny State apparatchiks go a lot further than wasting our money and not doing what they claim to be doing, they also inflict harm on others, they degrade the quality of life, they reduce the overall quotient of human happiness.

They are also absolutely sure they are right, so are impervious to any evidence or claim that what they do is counter-productive. In this respect they are similar to some secular zealots, such as born-again Christians or scientologists, which is why they appear so creepily virtuous. Yet, they do not subscribe to any particular ideological world view like, say, Marxism or Republicanism.

The architects of the Nanny State may draw their language and thinking from the same Third Way/post-modernist well but they don't share a common, binding ideology. What does bind them together, however, is the certainty that they are doing good. They are absolutely sure about that, which is probably why Tony Blair uses the term absolutely every other sentence.

Of course, there is no reasoning with such people because minds that have seen the light cannot be changed by evidence, argument or appeal. The only thing that changes them is a brighter light, a newer, trendier cause. In fact, it is dangerous to try to present evidence, argue or appeal to any ideologue of the Nanny State as this is the equivalent of just banging one's head against the wall. Such self-inflicted injuries do, however, qualify one for state-subsidised counselling or, even better, perhaps a no-win, no-fee deal to sue the Nanny State for negligence.

Every day we are confronted with cumbersome legislation telling us how to think, how to behave, and how to look after our 'health and safety'. None of it acknowledges that most people are possessed of a certain degree of common sense and can survive without constant interference. Unfortunately, accepting that people can live without the state's guiding influence would mean making half of those employed in the public sector redundant. All the 'Smoking Cessation Officers' and 'Five-a-Day Coordinators' would be forced to find something constructive to do in order to get a share of the Exchequer's income. They might become nurses or hospital orderlies, for example, and actually benefit people's health.

Instead, they waste public money on totally irrelevant schemes that more often than not hinder those they try to help. Simultaneously, their activities foster the belief that individuals need take no responsibility for their own lives. We are duped into believing that our lives are the responsibility of the state.

While, as has been argued, it is easy to laugh such schemes off as just another example of British eccentricity, it is dangerous to do so, because their implications are far-reaching. Once the ball has started rolling, there is little anyone can do to stop it, and the speed with which the nannying pervades every aspect of life is dizzying. Suddenly its influence has extended well beyond pointless warnings to keep out of the sun, and is finding its way into everything, from the 'regulations' governing the food that we eat, the 'definitions' of words that are deemed acceptable, to the undermining of the justice system, the stripping away of civil liberties, and the indoctrination of our children – which could take generations to heal.

Where the state can genuinely help the individual, it is clear that it should strive to do so. Where it can't, however, it should accept that fact. It serves no one to offer sound bites and half-hearted 'guidelines' in place of insight and solutions. A genuinely responsible state should concede that most people are quite capable of working their way through life without ill-informed ministerial guidance. Indeed, most of us would far prefer to be left alone. After all, more is gained from a life lived than a life prescribed.

It is all too easy to blame the increasing restrictions of civil liberties on politicians. Ultimately, however, this misses the point. Tony Blair, and ministers like Margaret Hodge and David Blunkett, may have ideas abhorrent to those who value individual freedom, but they are entitled to believe whatever they want. They are obviously not entitled to mislead the electorate in pursuit of the more absurd elements of their philosophy, but in our democracy this is exactly what they do. Many regard the failure to exercise one's right to vote as reprehensible. It is even more reprehensible to regard a government we voted in, and have the power to vote out, with apathy. We employ the government and we must share responsibility for its actions.

The nanny's traditional response to a spoiled child who thinks it 'unfair' that he is not allowed another scoop of ice-cream is to tell him that 'life is unfair'. Unfortunately, nannies are right. Life is unfair. Not everybody is born into great wealth and not everybody is born possessed of any particular beauty, for example. However, one great blessing that most citizens in the industrialised democracies are granted at birth is freedom. In democratic societies, people decide for themselves how they want to be governed. The awful truth is that most of us take this for granted and, so, do nothing about it.

Much of the developing world, especially those parts of it where fundamentalist religion still exerts a strong influence, believe that freedom, capitalism and democracy engender a dangerous decadence in Western societies. To a certain extent, this is true. Our decadence does not lie, however, in our licentiousness as we ogle pictures of topless women in the tabloids. Nor are we decadent because we occasionally have one too many after a night on the town or because we enjoy foreign holidays and fattening foods.

Our decadence lies in the fact that we have inherited one of the most fair, tolerant and decent societies yet conceived of – where equality of opportunity and the democratic principle are considered almost sacred, and for which generations have fought long and bloody wars – and yet we cannot be bothered to respect that legacy enough to protect it. The Nanny State has embarked on a process of removing our freedoms by stealth and we just ridicule it. Our laughter is sounding increasingly hollow, however.

The turnout for the 2001 election was just 59.2 per cent – the lowest in history, having collapsed from 71 per cent in 1997. New Labour have tried to use this fact to demonstrate the electorate's 'contentment' with their administration. However, a survey in the constituency of Liverpool Riverside, where only 34 per cent of constituents turned up to the polling booths, revealed that the rest 'couldn't see the point' of voting. Many even claimed that they 'didn't support' any of the main parties. The government tried to pretend that the low turnout was due to a 'trend' common in Western Democracies. It is a trend, however, bucked by the 81 per cent who participated in the Italian elections, and the 80–85 per cent of people who vote at elections in Scandinavia, Austria and Germany.

Tony Blair constantly reminds the nation that we must 'take responsibility' for our lives, but it is clearly to his advantage that we don't. The size of his party's majority allows him to get away with the more anti-democratic of his proposals. This is one of the failings of our political system, encapsulated by Disraeli when he observed ironically, 'No government can be long secure without a formidable opposition.' Too much power is bad for the government, bad for democracy and, ultimately, bad for us.

In the current situation politicians argue that legislation, which is quite clearly undemocratic, is democratic, because it is introduced by the party with the most seats. Redundant surveys of tiny sections of the public are used to justify legislation along the same lines. So a poll that shows that 70 per cent of the population are in favour of banning smoking in public, extrapolated from a sample of a few hundred people, is used to show that legislation banning smoking in public would be the democratically correct thing to do. Except that it wouldn't. You might as well ask one person whether they like celery, and then cite this 'poll' as proof that celery should be banned because 100 per cent of those polled were against it. This is no more ridiculous than the Nanny State's attitude. It is just presented sufficiently simply for its ridiculousness to be obvious.

The fundamental principle of a democracy is not that every law is subjected to a referendum or, even, that every law should be submitted to the public for approval. We vote to appoint a trusted representative to make informed decisions about policy on our behalf. He in turn is subject to the equal democratic duty to promote our chosen policies in the language of reason.

The responsibility of the voter, therefore, is to monitor how well his member of parliament is representing, under the democratic charter, his interests. If he fails to do so, he gets voted out, but not harangued every time he sanctions a policy the voter disagrees with. As Gladstone said, our business 'is not to govern the country but it is, if you think fit, to call to account those who do govern it'.

The New Labour government know this. However, under the pretence of 'accountability' they occasionally pretend that this is not so. They disingenuously wave the results of hastily conducted 'polls' around as evidence that they are behaving democratically. Such a political system is not democracy but ochlocracy, the rule of the mob.

One of the fundamental principles of a democracy is that, while every citizen has the vote, there are still mechanisms in place to protect the rights of minorities. Thomas Jefferson described this as a...

> ...sacred principle: that though the will of the majority is in all cases to prevail, that will, to be rightful, must be reasonable; that the minority possess their equal rights, which equal laws must protect, and to violate would be oppression.

This government puts great store by its devotion to the rights of minorities, which of course it should do, but it then cherry-picks a handful of minorities whose rights it strives to protect, at the expense of those whose votes it believes it will never win over. So the misguided pursuit of multiculturalism sees the government encouraging the nation to show respect and tolerance to particular groups of immigrants, while showing nothing but contempt and intolerance for those minorities who like to smoke cigarettes or hunt foxes.

Like a greedy and devious nanny who steals her charges' sweets when they are not looking, or the conjuror at their birthday parties who makes things magically 'appear' through sleight of hand, the government has used all manner of tricks to blind the electorate to the imposition of its controlling agenda. Through boredom, apathy and laziness, however, the electorate have yawned and let them do so, and if it were not for the legacy that will be left to our children, the country would deserve what it has coming to it.

There is an apocryphal story about G. K. Chesterton in which a leading London newspaper was supposed to have posed the question 'What is wrong with Britain Today?', to a number of recognised writers and politicians. The usual volley of replies came back, with various thinkers from different positions on the political spectrum, arguing that the conditions of the workers were letting the country down, or that the strains of the War were too great on the economy. Were a modern day newspaper to ask the same question, a similarly predictable collection of responses would doubtless be received. The influence of Brussels would no doubt be criticised by one faction, while the influence of America would be criticised by another. General Sir Huffton-Puffton Bart. would no doubt write in saying that the problem today was the youth and the coloureds, while some crusty-haired animal rights campaigner would probably blame everything on the toffs, the 'system' and those who wear patent leather shoes.

No doubt a number of people would make the snide and ill-considered conclusion that what was wrong with the country was the government or, even more specifically, the Prime Minister.

It is unlikely, however, that anyone would supply an answer as damning, insightful and conclusive as Chesterton's. In answer to the question 'What is wrong with Britain today?' he replied simply, 'Dear Sir, I am.'

NOTES

Introduction
Nanny knows best

'Stay Indoors...', Department of Health Press Release,
7 August, 2003.

'We should not expect the state...', quoted in *Commanding Heights* by Daniel Yergin and Joseph Stanislaw, Simon and Schuster, 2002.

'We support a market economy...', *Europe, The Third Way / Die Neue Mitte,* Tony Blair and Gerhard Schroeder, 7 June 1999.

'...the vagaries of the individual', in a speech at the *Children - Do They Count?* Conference, 18 November 2003.

1 Nanny's family tree

'..I desire from my heart...' Oliver Cromwell, John Buchan, Thomas Nelson & sons, 1936.

'...meddling in their private affairs...', idem.

'Whatever is done for men or classes...', The Forging of the Modern State, EJ Evans, Longam, 2001(3rd ed)

'..not a wounded Russia only, but a poisoned...', Churchill, Roy Jenkins, Pan, 2001.

'...was not rigidly dogmatic...' idem.

2 If at first you don't succeed...

'Individuals cannot protect themselves...', The Times, 22 October, 2003.

'...like there is in abattoirs', BBC News, 6 August, 2001

'You believe that reality...', 1984, George Orwell, Penguin 1990 edition.

'...seventeenth-century society mistreated women', a professor at Duke University, quoted by Margaret Thatcher in a speech at the International Conservative Congress, December. 22, 1997.

'We believe that it is respectable to be blind...' Resolution 93-01 (1999) of the National Federation of the Blind.

'I'm just a white boy called the Deputy CC...', quoted in BBC News, 27 April, 2004.

'So look, shall I buy this top...', *Britkid* (www.britkid.org.).

'We mean the bonds of culture...', BNP website (www.bnp.org.uk).

'There is no aspect of African culture...', speech at the Civil Service Race Equality Network Annual Lecture, 26 April, 2004.

'What this man did to a German computer expert...', *San Francisco Chronicle*, 21 December 2003.

'To give worms and slugs protection...', *Daily Telegraph*, 11 July, 2004

'...it is the poorer...who are most visibly damaged', The Guardian, 1 January, 2000.

'Individuals cannot protect themselves from bio-terrorism...' Professor John Ashton.

'Oddly, when deconstructionists required appendectomies...' *Hooking Up*, Tom Wolfe, Picador, 2002.

3 Health risks and safety hazard

'It looks easy on TV...', BBC News, 21 April, 2000.

'The Nanny State gone absolutely berserk...', *Daily Telegraph,* 23 May, 2004.

'Obesity could overtake smoking as the most...', *Daily Telegraph,* 6 April, 2004.

'Two million Britons are so underfed...', *The Mirror*, 12 November, 2002.

'Eating junk food harms the memory...' *Daily Mail,* 5 April, 2004.

'A growing number of household pets...' *Daily Express,* 12 June, 2004.

'The sight of amputees...', House of Commons Select Committee Third Health Report, 10 May, 2004.

'...distract attention from the root point', *The Times,* 14 June, 2004.

'We have transformed the labour...' Welfare State Conference on Economic Policies, 3 December, 1993.

'...irreparable damage to the way we police', *The Telegraph,* 28 June, 2003.

4 Monsters under the bed

'**We can live in a world...**', interview on LWT's *Dimbleby*, 11 November 2001.

'**Violent video films may in part...**', *Guardian,* November 25, 1993.

'**For the sake of all our kids...**', *Sun,* 26 November 1993.

'**We dismiss any link...**', *Guardian*, 13 April 1994.

'**Our homes have been penetrated by garbage...**', *Sun,* 25 November 1993.

'**Ugly manifestation...**', quoted in *The Blair Revolution: Can New Labour Deliver?* By Peter Mandelson and Roger Liddle, Faber and Faber (February 1996).

'**It often happens, we are aware...**', Thomas Wright: 'On a Possible Popular Culture', *Contemporary Review* (July 1881)
'**I think one's got to make a difference...**', interview with Radio Five Live, 19 December 1996.

'**The difference between art and child pornography...**', *The Sun,* 9 March, 2004.

'**If every person who had a sexual interest...**', BBC News, 9 December, 2003.

'**...not nearly impossible, impossible.**', quoted in *The Observer,* 28 December, 2003.

'**Put the cart before the horse in pretending...**', ibid.

'**I happen to believe that once...**', *The Scotsman*, 5 May, 2004.

'**An ID card is best equipped...**', *The Guardian,* 13 May 2004.

'**You are adding to the nation's critical infrastructure...**', Select Committee on Home Affairs Fourth Report, 20 July 2004.

'**Fail every practical and principled measure...**', *The Observer,* 9 May, 2004.

'**My anxiety is that we don't sleepwalk...**', *The Times,* 19 August, 2004.

5 There, there, it's not your fault...

'**We are today a nation...in a state of shock...**', Downing Street Press Release, 31 August 1997.

'**Crucial characteristic of all therapy culture...**', Frank Furedi, *Therapy Culture,* Routledge, 2003.

'**...large over-estimate of the number of those needing treatment**', Derek Summerfield, 'War and mental health: a brief overview', *British Medical Journal* 2000.

'**Effectively, the psychosocial model involves...**', Vanessa Pupavac, 'Therapeutic Governance: Psychosocial Intervention and Trauma Risk Management', Disasters 2001.

'**I feel very strongly that individuals...**', *Daily Mail,* 22 June, 2004.

'**If people can prove someone else was at fault...**', *Daily Telegraph,* 20 April, 2004.

'**Has your child had an accident at school?...**' *The Observer,* 20 May, 2004.

'**It means that less adventurous children...**', *The Observer,* 30 May, 2004.

'**It would be nice to think that sufficient funds...**' *The Guardian,* 12 March 2004.

'**We need to inject a degree of honesty...**', Science Media Centre Press Release, 2004.

'**The food industry is being viewed...**', *The Guardian*, 27 May, 2004.

6 Sentence first, verdict afterwards

'**The scheme is not rocket science...**', *Observer,* 2 May, 2004.

'**...the life chances of children**', Speech on Anti-Social Behaviour at the QEII centre, 14 October, 2003.

'**...condemn a little more and understand a little less.**', *Daily Mail*, 22 February 1993

'**... a modern civic society,**', *Observer,* November 10, 2002.

'**We need to create a responsible society...**' BBC News, 29 November, 2000

'**People do not want a return to old prejudices...**' Speech on Five-Year Crime Strategy, 19 July, 2004.

7 Come with me, my pretties...

'**Children – *Do They Count?***', The Congress Centre, 18 November, 2003.

'**Education is a partnership...**', *The Guardian,* 27 September, 2000.

'**I do believe that the right to smack...**', *The Telegraph,* 10 December, 2000.

'**Children are being legally hit right now!**', www.childrenareunbeatable.org.uk.

'**We are equipping our nation for a world of tomorrow...**', *The*

Guardian, 27 September, 2000.

'I see no point in putting extra money...', *The Guardian,*
17 July, 2002.

'And how old are you, my dear?',   David Blunkett, *On a Clear Day*, Michael O'Mara (1995).

'...is not properly assessed across all schools', *The Guardian,* 11 July, 2003.

'...bit about oral sex for avoiding pregnancy', *The Guardian,* 21 February, 2003.

CONCLUSION
Children should be seen and not heard

'Too much power is bad for the government', The Oxford Book of Quotations (Benjamin Disraeli)

'...sacred principle: that though the will of the majority...'
Thomas Jefferson, 1st Inaugaural 1801.

INDEX